Advance Praise

"Rob Weinhold has captured in this one book what it took me 28 books to communicate to CEO's."

—Dr. Joseph Mancuso, founder of CEO Clubs International, ceoclubs.org and ceoclubsworldwide.com

"Having taught both crisis management and resiliency to business executives and public safety leaders through Hopkins' Police Executive Leadership Program (PELP), this book offers tremendous perspective and is a clear resource for all leaders who want to understand the nuances of survival during life's most critical times."

—Dr. Katherine Wilson, Johns Hopkins Carey Business School

"As a record-breaking professional driver who has smashed several transcontinental driving records in various vehicles, I've learned that preparation, endurance and will are the keys to coming out victorious in high-risk and high-intensity situations. Rob's knowledge offered in this book is critical to avoiding and surviving issues that test your personal or professional grit."

—Carl Reese, endurance driver and Guinness World Record holder

"Whether a top executive or entry level employee, sooner or later, through no fault of your own, your business or personal reputation will be tested. To preserve your good name, immediate action must be taken. Weinhold's deep knowledge and expert perspective is clear—and, the key takeaways are right on point. This is a must read for anyone who wants to protect their most critical asset over time, their reputation."

—William Davis, Business Strategist and retired Fortune 100
     Executive

"In my 30 plus years as a television news executive, I've seen peoples' stories implode both on and off-camera, particularly when they're attempting to manage controversial issues. The real life situations and strategies detailed in this book are invaluable to those who have to make the tough decisions when the world is watching."

—Joe DeFeo, ABC7/NewsChannel8 Washington, DC

"...the ultimate primer every successful business leader and executive should have in their arsenal. Weinhold shares lessons learned and best practices from decades of experience in a concise and entertaining manner with real world examples that will keep the reader engaged and looking for more."

—L. Content McLaughlin, J.D., LL.M., Best Lawyers in
     America and 50 Women of Power and Influence designee

"Immensely interesting book from one of the best in the crisis leadership industry. Weinhold has seen it all...from volatile local controversies to being a CNN commentator on issues of national importance. Crisis? Weinhold and his team is your solution!"

—Leonard Sipes, former federal senior spokesperson, 35 years
     of media relations experience

"Rob has a tremendous amount of professional experience, across multiple industries, which he describes perfectly throughout this book. The book isn't about Rob, it is about Rob using his experiences to help others and ensure others are learning from the life lessons he and others endured through many years of challenges and unexpected situations. We all believe that you can only control what you can control, and you must take the necessary small steps to be effective in life. There is so much we can learn from other people; Rob is the king of stepping back, evaluating and finding ways to improve and lessons to be learned."

—Ben Leigh, Professional & Amateur Sports Marketing Executive

The Art of
Crisis Leadership

The Art of
Crisis Leadership

Rob Weinhold
with Kevin Cowherd

Apprentice House
Loyola University Maryland
Baltimore, Maryland

First Edition

Printed in the United States of America

Hardcover ISBN: 978-1-62720-112-4
Paperback ISBN: 978-1-62720-113-1
E-book ISBN: 978-1-62720-114-8

Cover Design: Brandon Lee Beach
Internal Design: Apprentice House
Photo of Author by Josie Hankey
Editorial Development: Karl Dehmelt

Published by Apprentice House

Apprentice House
Loyola University Maryland
4501 N. Charles Street
Baltimore, MD 21210
410.617.5265 • 410.617.2198 (fax)
www.ApprenticeHouse.com
info@ApprenticeHouse.com

I dedicate this milestone to Cindy, Timothy, Garrett and Brendan.

Without your lifelong support, interest, enthusiasm and encouragement, nothing I have ever accomplished would have meaning or would have even been possible.

I am gratefully indebted to each of you for making my life complete.

Acknowledgments

In any job I've ever had, whether walking around with an oily gas can and Craftsman push mower as a 12-year-old to revamping core business verticals at a high level, I've always approached life with an entrepreneurial spirit. How does one make something bigger, faster, stronger—in other words, optimize it? And, what was it that the very best leaders did to drive results, real results? After all, it's not what you take on, it's what you accomplish!

I have never been opposed to calculated risk and generally had a knack for thinking big and mobilizing resources. It was with this mindset that I nervously embarked on the biggest professional risk of my life—starting my own company in 2009—after having worked really hard for many years making others look good, and making them lots of money. As an admirer of sound leadership, I had often wondered why I'd turn on the news each night and see once proud leaders recklessly sabotaging their own careers. Why was it that so many behaved irresponsibly when faced with crisis or controversy? Why did so many say and do the wrong things and end up being judged so harshly in the court of public opinion? Reputation matters, and so many of these leaders didn't have a clue. Either they were getting really bad advice, or they were not following the good advice they were given—neither of which are acceptable.

After driving executive strategy for many years, I knew leadership teams generally did a really good job of advancing their own missions. But when issues of adversity or crisis threw them off course, there was generally no one at the helm, with deep experience, who could get the organization back on track and drive favorable outcomes for years to come. I knew there was a marketplace gap.

This gave me an idea. And Fallston Group was born.

When I saw Kevin Cowherd walking out of Baltimore business magnate Ed Hale's office more than a year ago, it was a happy accident. I was managing a major client issue and Kevin was coming down the homestretch with his latest book, a biography of Hale called—"Hale Storm". Kevin had wrapped-up a 32-year career as a columnist and feature writer for The Baltimore Sun, and was now a full-time author. As fate would have it, writing a book was on my life-long list of things to do, and a book about crisis leadership seemed perfect for these ominous and uncertain times. And from this, a terrific collaboration was born. After developing the book's concept and managing my many ideas, Kevin was masterful at bringing my thoughts to life. He worked relentlessly with me to produce a manuscript that I hope has tremendous value and offers meaningful insights to leaders at every level. Thank you, Kevin.

Most importantly, I must acknowledge those folks who told the stories that form the core of this book, those people who opened their hearts and minds to relive their darkest days so that others could learn from their experiences: Denise Whiting, Ed Norris, Jack and Jackie Milani, Kevin Byrne, Stephen Amos, Mark Curtis, Joe Hart, Gerry Sandusky, J.P. Snyder, Colin Goddard, Jim and Joanne Hock and Bert Lebhar.

They told their stories with passion; each experience was emotional. This book is about real people and real life lessons. It would have been impossible to produce without the generosity of spirit and unfailing cooperation of those listed above.

There were many others who supported this project in ways both large and small: Josie Hankey, Jessica Paret, Jennifer Fuson, Content McLaughlin, Tim Weinhold, Frank Barile, Paul Bailey, Kristi Frisch, Joe DeFeo, Ragina Averella, Jim Workmeister and Kevin Atticks, director of Apprentice House Press.

During this chaotic time, the extended Fallston Group team—and its stable of experts—was still able to move our corporate offices from Harford County, Md., to the Canton neighborhood of Baltimore, work at an incredibly high level and continue to over-deliver for those who trust us with their futures. I am eternally grateful for your collective selflessness and dedication.

Yes, we help and serve others during life's most critical times daily—it's baked into our DNA. It's my honor to work shoulder-to-shoulder with the extended Fallston Group team.

On a more personal level, I'd like to thank my parents, Robert Winway and Etna Anderson Weinhold. While they are now looking down upon us, their incredible love and support never wavered. I draw strength and wisdom from each of you daily.

Lastly, there are those who enter your life for reasons that are sometimes explainable, but many times not. They are motivating influences that shape your thinking and drive you to succeed—not because of what they say, but how they live their lives.

They set the example and teach through their actions. Thank you, Pat Casperson, for being the foundation in the lives around you and for selflessly putting others before yourself, always. You are a role model and inspiration.

Foreword

"A rising tide lifts all boats," the old adage says. It was easy to make profits in the stock market when the technology boom was driving all stocks higher. It was easy to make a killing in real estate when real estate seemed to be appreciating with no ceiling in site. And it was easy to be an effective leader in prosperous times when even poor decisions seemed to be self-correcting. The true test of leadership, however, is the same as the true test of friendship: crisis, adversity.

Other than the study of religion, the study of leadership may represent the oldest recorded intellectual pursuit in human history, but surprisingly few books focus on crisis leadership. If ever there was time to study crisis leadership, it's now! Global affairs seem in disarray, with conflict being fueled from Russia, ISIS, North Korea, Iran, and China. Within North America, drug cartels appear to have extraordinary influence. In the United States, financial markets are experiencing unprecedented volatility, many large urban centers are undergoing economic hardship, the quality and availability of healthcare seems questionable, normal political discourse has turned into paralyzing vitriol, racial tensions have increased, and the gap between the wealthy and middle class has widened. Admittedly, volatility is part of the human condition. There will be peaks and valleys in the trajectory of every human endeavor. Having conflict and experiencing setbacks are to be expected, but what is needed in the wake of such adversity is crisis leadership that fosters RESILIENCE! Whether the crises are personal, organizational, or communal, leadership that promotes resilience will be that factor that determines success from failure.

I am no stranger to human resilience. In 1992, I was asked to assist in fostering the resilience of the social fabric of the country of Kuwait after the Iraqi invasion and the Gulf War liberation. After the terrorist attacks of September 11, 2001, as a consultant to the NYPD and the New Jersey State Police, I trained first responders to be resilient and later assisted large organizations in being resilient in the wake of the financial crash of 2008. I taught organizations to foster an *organizational culture of resilience*. I continue to do that today as a professor at The Johns Hopkins University and as a consultant to many large organizations. I've authored 20 books including *Secrets of Resilient Leadership* (2009) and *Stronger: Discover the Resilience You Need to Succeed! (2015)* that share my experiences in 33 countries on six continents as I've tried to promote human resilience in the wake of adversity. In those experiences, I've observed that wherever organizations and communities successfully rebound after a crisis, it is largely because of extraordinary crisis leadership—leadership that fosters resilience. Whether working in the Middle East, Oklahoma City, New York City, or working with elite first responders or U.S. Navy SEALs, I've seen crisis leadership as an essential of organizational resilience.

The book you are about to read is written by Rob Weinhold, Founder and Chief Executive of Fallston Group and a pioneer in the field of crisis leadership. I've worked with Rob on numerous occasions and witnessed first-hand his masterful ability to snatch victory from the jaws of defeat in the wake of great adversity. Now Rob shares the richness of his experience in a book that is a unique blend of entertainment and priceless practicality. The book effortlessly glides from one example to another with very important lessons learned. Anyone who is in a leadership position, or who aspires to leadership, should read this most valuable contribution. For as any wise leader knows, it's not IF crisis strikes, but merely a matter of WHEN. Will you be prepared when it does? The lessons in this book will prepare you to lead before, during, and after a crisis.

George S. Everly, Jr., PhD, FAPM
The Johns Hopkins University

"Glass, China, and Reputation, are easily cracked, and never well mended."

—Benjamin Franklin

Introduction

A Life-Changing Experience on the Mean Streets of Baltimore

It was a beautiful fall morning in September of 1992. Back then, I was a young Baltimore police officer on patrol in the Southeastern District of the city, right off Lombard Street near Corned Beef Row and the legendary Attman's Deli.

I was checking out a house that had reportedly been burglarized when I got the strangest feeling. When you work a neighborhood for any length of time, you develop a sense of when something is out of place, when the rhythm of the streets seems off.

I saw a car speeding in the wrong direction down a one-way street in front of the Flag House high-rise. I saw a housing police officer running. My instincts told me something was very wrong, although I didn't know what.

I knew that a fellow officer, a young, street-smart, energetic colleague named Jimmy Young, was working plainclothes that day, doing drug buys in the projects. As I looked up at one of the nearby public housing high-rise buildings, I saw what appeared to be a body slumped against a chain-link fence on the third floor.

I could tell it was a black man, wearing the same clothes Jimmy had worn that day. I knew because I'd been joking with him that morning that he was dressed like the skinheads who skateboarded in Fells Point. Jimmy and I had worked closely together in the same squad. We worked-out in the bare-bones, iron pit gym on the second floor of the district and had an easy relationship. He had an infectious smile that captivated everyone he met—he was a great cop. Nervously, I prayed it wasn't him laying against that fence as I began running toward the building in full sprint.

Suddenly, my police radio crackled. A faint voice said an officer had been shot—I knew the voice belonged to Jimmy's partner, whom he'd been riding with that day.

I ran into the high-rise, which was very dark, and up the stairwell. I was convinced I'd run into the person or persons who'd shot Jimmy coming down, so my service weapon was drawn. I headed quickly, but cautiously, up the stairs. Anyone who has worn a badge for a living understands this unique challenge: I was going from bright sunlight into a very dark building. Until your eyes adjust, it can be very unnerving, particularly when gunfights and street violence were the norm in the streets I patrolled for a living.

I was the first uniformed officer to reach Jimmy's side. I could see he'd been shot in the head. His eyes were half-closed. He appeared to be lifeless. I had been to a lot of homicide scenes and this looked like another, except this time, it was Jimmy.

The next step would normally have been to call Homicide, then chalk-off the body. But an officer named Vince Moore arrived behind me in seconds.

Vince had been a paramedic in the military. He immediately began CPR on Jimmy as I got on the radio and gave tactical information and direction to responding units about what had happened, where to go and what we were looking for.

Everything was happening at lightning speed.

Suspects were on the loose. The crime scene needed to be secured.

Witnesses needed to be located. The Homicide unit needed to be notified. And an ambulance was on its way and would need directions to our location. People were yelling and screaming—it was a very emotional and unsettling time.

My major assigned me to accompany Jimmy to Shock Trauma. After a quick ride through cross-town traffic with sirens wailing (motorized units had shut down a lane for the ambulance on Lombard Street), Jimmy was now on a gurney in the world's best trauma unit. If there was any chance to save Jimmy's life, it would happen here.

There were at least 12 doctors and nurses around him that I could see. I stood about 20 feet away, helpless. The scene of the shooting, which had initially appeared so loud and chaotic, had been replaced by a team of highly-trained medical professionals working with quiet, creative intensity. I could hear nothing but the rapid movement of medical professionals coupled with the familiar sounds of medical monitors.

It was like going from a raucous carnival into an utterly silent library.

I stood there marveling at the efficiency of these dedicated men and women when a nurse approached and said: "Listen, when he dies, we're going to notify you, so you can notify your superiors and handle this however you need to."

All I could think was: of all the people who loved Jimmy in this world, I was the only one here right now who knew him and cared about him as a colleague and friend. We were just laughing a few hours earlier—how could this be happening? Life changed so quickly.

It was an incredibly powerful moment, made even more powerful when another nurse showed me the results of Jimmy's CAT scan. The bullet had grazed his skull, but also cracked it, sending shards of bone fragments into his brain.

Things looked incredibly grim for Jimmy—I was mentally preparing for the worst as the gravity of the day was beginning to set in.

Soon, the docs and nurses seemed to stop working on him

altogether. It was as if they had run out of things to do, procedures to try. When someone spotted a slight, involuntary movement of his foot—WHAM!—they were all over him again, working feverishly.

The bottom line: Jimmy Young survived.

He was in rehabilitation for a long time, healing and learning to deal with his brain injuries while living a "new normal." All of us in the squad had to deal with something too: the post-traumatic stress that invariably affects those who are a part of a terrifying, life-changing event. We didn't know we had PTSD, but as it turns out, all of us who had a piece of that day's events felt the impact in ways we never imagined or realized.

Everyone who had a hand in what happened to Jimmy—from dispatchers to responding officers to unit commanders—took part in a group "therapy" session.

One evening, some 25 of us sat in a circle and talked about the events stemming from his shooting. We talked about the role each of us had played—our feelings, emotions, the whole nine yards.

It was incredibly curative and beneficial. Most cops, after a shooting of one of their own, would think: *OK, we've gotta go out and drink and talk about this.*

But this was an incredible and very emotional exercise that lasted nearly four hours. The therapeutic value far out-weighed anything you could get from throwing back beers and shots in a dimly-lit bar. (Which isn't to say we didn't end up there afterward.)

What the Jimmy Young shooting taught me from a crisis leadership standpoint is that when a crisis occurs, no matter how traumatic the event, everyone needs to understand his or her role and stay in their own lane. This doesn't happen without proper policies, planning, training and execution.

Yet, many organizations don't have the very basic, and most foundational element of crisis preparedness in place: namely, a practiced, actionable plan.

From the police department perspective, all of these moving

parts—responding officers, those who canvass for witnesses, who preserve the crime scene, who investigate the crime, who work Homicide, who direct traffic, who dispatch calls—must come together for a singular, life-saving mission.

From a medical perspective, similar coordination must occur on the street by medics, the Shock Trauma team and rehabilitation centers. If all of these various police and healthcare personnel don't perform their roles with precision and efficiency during a crisis, heroes like Jimmy Young die.

In many ways, a parallel can be drawn about how worldwide organizations must prepare for and navigate through crisis; how they must create organizational muscle memory so they're ready to meet the moment. Whether it's a social media attack, court of public opinion issue, data breach, stakeholder relations issue, investigation, litigation, product recall, active shooter situation, or any other issue of adversity, leaders must be prepared for every eventuality. The first order of leadership is to provide a safe place to work. A very basic human need is physical and emotional safety—without safety, performance and productivity is dramatically decreased.

There are many "how to" references and books on crisis planning, management and recovery. However, my goal with this book is to tell real stories, with raw emotion, about how true leaders prepared for, managed, and recovered from crisis, so that their organizations not only survived, but thrived. I'll also talk about the mistakes that both individuals and companies tend to make under duress, mistakes that can set them back years and alter their lives forever.

Crises cost time, money, customers and careers, and in the worst-case scenarios, lives. In these increasingly uncertain, often chaotic times where anyone with a recording device and internet connection can wreak havoc on your personal or professional brand, the issue is not *if* a crisis will hit, but *when.*

Yet crisis leadership is an art, not a science. Many of the decisions I've made as a crisis leader can't be easily explained and are often based on instinct while factoring dozens of nuances that are quickly processed and acted upon.

Certainly, my background has helped me develop this innate sense.

As a uniformed patrol officer in a major metropolitan city, I saw much of the best and worst that life has to offer. I saw a side of humanity that was both motivating and deflating. Promoted to Public Affairs Director of the Baltimore PD after my sworn service days, my job entailed briefing the news media and many other leaders daily on a seemingly endless list of volatile urban issues—pervasive crime, allegations of police brutality, charges of racial inequity, public safety policy and politics. I learned very quickly to be politically astute, but not political. The waters of Baltimore politics are some of the most treacherous in the country, as countless out-of-town leaders have confided.

I also served as chief of staff for the U.S. Department of Justice and as a senior executive within the Maryland governor's office. I've worked on the core executive leadership team at all three levels of government and, in the private sector, on the core executive team of Ripken Baseball, headed by Hall of Famer Cal Ripken Jr., and former major leaguer Bill Ripken.

In 2009, I continued my career mission of helping people and organizations during life's most critical times by launching Fallston Group (www.FallstonGroup.com), a Baltimore-based crisis management and communications firm designed to help organizations prepare for, navigate through and recover from issues of sensitivity, adversity and crisis. The experienced team I surround myself with has a unique passion for helping others through life's most critical times—it's baked into our collective DNA.

For more than two decades, dating back to that fateful autumn morning in Baltimore's Southeastern District and the tragic shooting of Officer Jimmy Young, I've studied how individuals, small businesses, large corporations and governments handle difficult times. Life comes at you fast sometimes and coping is almost never easy.

The case studies, lessons learned and instructional points contained in this book are designed to help readers face their fears, learn from the experiences of others and, ultimately, turn short-term adversity into long-term advantage.

Many of the case studies in this book involve people I've worked with personally. They have agreed to tell their stories with the hope that their trials might help others. There are many other public, private and governmental clients I've had the honor of working with, and I am grateful for their continued trust and confidence. I remain intrigued by their relentless sense of perseverance and resilience during life's most critical times. They are an inspiration to us all.

1

The Anatomy of Crisis

It was the scandal known as "Dieselgate" that brought Volkswagen to the brink of disaster.

For decades, the German auto giant had enjoyed a sterling reputation for manufacturing eco-friendly cars designed to the highest standards and beloved by an almost fanatically-loyal segment of the car-buying public.

But that all changed in September of 2015, when the company was accused of secretly installing software on as many as 11 million of its diesel vehicles that allowed them to evade emissions standards.

The backlash was swift and predictable.

More than a third of Volkswagen's market value vanished immediately. Its CEO, Martin Winterkorn, was forced to step down after saying he was "shocked" by the details of the scandal and "stunned that misconduct on such a scale was possible" in the company. His departure further cemented the leadership principle that you can, at times, delegate authority, but never accountability.

Volkswagen's new chief executive, Matthias Mueller, earnestly assured all who would listen that the company would "do everything to win back the trust of our customers, our employees, our partners, investors and the whole public."

With the cost of repairs needed to undo the rigged software

expected to reach into the billions of dollars, some German leaders feared it could wreak havoc on the country's economy.

In what seemed like the blink of an eye, one of the most prominent companies in the world plunged deeply into crisis—its brand severely damaged. And, as of this writing, there was no way to tell what the company would look like when it rebounds. According to a research analyst quoted in *Forbes* magazine, total estimates for lost business, recalling, fixing and compensating U.S. VW diesel car owners and government and state fines could range as high as $50 billion.

"We are facing a long trudge and a lot of hard work," Mueller told company leaders, according to media reports. "We will only be able to make progress in steps. And there will be setbacks."

The dictionary defines crisis in many ways: a turning point; an emotionally-significant event; something that can bring about radical change, pain, stress, disordered function, instability and highly-undesirable outcomes.

We know crises can be natural, like an earthquake, or human-induced, like war. Crises can be sudden or smoldering, high-impact or low-impact. Sometimes organizations and people recover from them. Many times, they do not.

Crises can take on many forms: data breach, social media attack, negative press, natural disaster, bankruptcy, crime, litigation, investigation, compliance issues, employee relations complications, job loss, labor unrest, audit sanction, IT issues, board dissension, poorly-managed mergers, environmental damage, workplace violence, whistle blowers, IP theft, rumors, death, terrorism, war, riots, accidents, homelessness, health issues, strikes, product recall, regulatory shifts, competitive disruption, hostile takeovers, abuse, poor leadership transition, and discrimination—to name some of the more prominent ones.

Life is a complex struggle at times, with a seemingly high level of unpredictability.

But one thing is certain: crisis *will* strike.

It's not a matter of *if.* It's a matter of *when.*

In recent years alone, the number of "big brands" that have found themselves in crisis is staggering. Toyota, Penn State, Goldman Sachs, BP, Target, Sony, Uber, GM, Malaysia Airlines, the NFL, Starbucks, Chipotle, The Susan G. Komen Breast Cancer Foundation, Bill Cosby, Paula Deen, Jared Fogle, Johnny Manziel and dozens of others have faced serious reputational issues that have cost them tremendous amounts of time, money, customers, and, ultimately, their careers.

In my decades of managing crisis—the overwhelming number of them man-made—I've found premeditated crises are deeply rooted in the issues of power, money, sex and revenge.

As wonderful as the human spirit is, there is often another side to some of us, a side in which these addictive triggers become more important than life itself. And, sadly, it's generally those who orbit the lives of the afflicted person—and depend on him or her emotionally, financially or spiritually—who suffer the most when that person's life unravels, whether the issue is personal or professional.

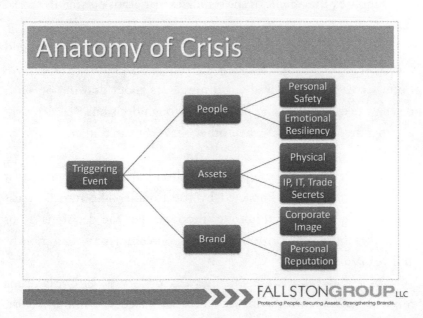

The case of the Volkswagen emissions crisis followed the well-worn path of many corporate crises before it, with a triggering event quickly impacting the organization's people, assets and brand.

Crises such as the Volkswagen scandal bring leadership and employees under intense scrutiny, with many losing their jobs, forcing them into professional and personal ruin.

Volkswagen's assets took a huge hit, as its recalled fleet of cars had to be retro-fitted with new emissions software, costing millions of dollars—and millions, if not billions, more will be spent in fines and litigation.

Finally, the Volkswagen brand may continue to diminish as valuation decreases and thoughtful consumers buy elsewhere. Where the floor ultimately is, no one knows.

No one can say with certainty when or where a crisis will occur. However, we can become more predictive and plan for the inevitable, which is why a true crisis leader is invaluable.

In many cases, a sound crisis leader can turn adversity into advantage simply by the way he or she stabilizes then leads during life's most difficult times.

An experienced crisis leader is one who operates with speed and precision at the intersection of leadership, strategy and communications. Crisis leadership is about instinct. It's about drawing on one's diverse life experiences and making the tough decisions that can help a company or individual when others have retreated in confusion or denial.

Effective crisis leadership is focused on building long-term trust with each stakeholder impacted by the trouble. The futurist crisis leader must be able to think far ahead, so that the decisions he or she makes today will positively influence outcomes for weeks, months and years to come.

Crisis leadership is not for the weak or indecisive. Crisis teams must be built to withstand turbulence, embrace risk and build trust. They *must* turn adversity into advantage—quality of life is in the balance.

Simply put, anyone can lead when times are good. But as former heavyweight boxer Mike Tyson eloquently put it: "Everyone has a plan 'til they get punched in the mouth."

True leaders, though, emerge when a crisis is at its very worst.

Don't miss your leadership moment!

2

The Unrelenting Surge of Community Pushback, Hon

Denise Whiting was a strong, accomplished woman who found herself desperate for help when she called Fallston Group during the hot Baltimore summer of 2011. I took her call that particular evening from an ice cream parlor parking lot in Long Beach Island, New Jersey, near one of my favorite fishing holes. I could immediately sense the pain and despair in her voice.

A successful restaurateur in the quirky, blue-collar Baltimore neighborhood of Hampden, her life had turned upside down over time and was reaching an unmanageable stage.

Now, her chest hurt so badly that she was afraid she'd suffered a heart attack. Without warning, she would lapse into crying jags that left her feeling shaken and vulnerable.

She feared for her life, going so far as to sleep with a shotgun under her bed, not knowing if her bad dreams in the middle of the night were reality or not.

What had happened to cause such anguish to this otherwise stalwart and proud businesswoman?

Simply put, she'd been blind-sided by a crisis, with a root cause that appeared almost laughable—if the consequences weren't so dire.

Her sin?

As the owner of the popular eatery Cafe Hon, a fixture on 36th Street in Baltimore since its opening in 1992, Whiting had dared to trademark the term "Hon" in order to protect her business interests.

Based on the advice of legal counsel, she'd been doing this for years, acquiring the rights to the term for restaurant services, retail services and T-shirts sold at her Hon boutique next door. Many other businesses had engaged in similar moves.

But "Hon" was a beloved local colloquialism—a cheerful term of endearment used by seemingly every waitress and hairdresser in town for decades. And once the media got hold of the story in late 2010—*Who is this selfish, greedy woman ripping off a cherished piece of Bawlmer culture?*—the backlash was swift and unrelenting.

Whiting's initial explanation of why she had trademarked Hon—and her first halting apologies about causing such a fuss—drew ridicule. Even though Whiting explained that she was merely doing what every sharp business person does—protecting her business interests through trademarking—she didn't realize the regional ire this move would provoke. Soon, protestors were demonstrating outside her restaurant holding signs that said "HONicide: Life on 36th Street" and "You Can't Trademark our Culture, Hon."

Yes, the community was pushing back—hard.

It didn't end there. She was bullied and threatened on social media, particularly on two Facebook pages called "Boycott Cafe Hon" and "No One Owns Hon, Hon."

In addition, she was blasted on the pages of *City Paper* and *The Baltimore Sun. Sun* columnist Dan Rodricks slammed her for a "crass effort to own a Baltimore regionalism," adding "Hon isn't unique to Denise Whiting, no matter how special she wants us to believe she is."

One lunatic Whiting hater even took to popping his head into Cafe Hon during business hours and screaming "NO ONE OWNS HON!" Not exactly a soothing accompaniment to a nice meal.

Her fellow merchants on "The Avenue" had also turned against her. And there was talk of a boycott of HonFest, the annual Whiting-founded homage to Baltimore women of a bygone era who favored beehive hair-dos, cats-eye glasses and housecoats. HonFest was a financial boon to the area. Tens of thousands of people attended this event on an annual basis. Now Whiting was being accused of changing the vendor rules, mainly with her request that Cafe Hon retain exclusive rights to the sale of cats-eye sunglasses.

Clearly, Denise Whiting's world was unraveling with astonishing speed.

Her business was tanking because of all the negative publicity. She had to lay off staff and withdraw $60,000 from her retirement fund to meet payroll. And the personal toll was devastating. She was hurt, humiliated and exhausted beyond measure.

"I contemplated suicide," she recalled. "I was so devastated. I remember standing in my bathroom and thinking: 'I could just end all this.' Because I couldn't take it. And it wouldn't go away. Everything I spent my last 21 years working on (was) now just non-existent."

My role as a crisis leadership expert was to quickly earn her trust, instill a sense of confidence and give her hope that there was a way out of this terrible mess. I had to be strong—for Denise and those that depended on her and the business.

The bottom line was that Denise was in a bunker and was refusing to come out, at least metaphorically speaking. Cafe Hon was no longer a safe haven, as folks would come into her restaurant during business hours and yell profanities.

Contributing to her problems was the fact that Denise was making no public statements about the Hon trademark and HonFest issues. She was not controlling the message or being heard. She was the neighborhood outcast and no one cared what she had to say.

Instead, the media, business community and assorted haters in Hampden and elsewhere were telling her story for her. It was a classic example of a lesson I've preached for years: "If you don't tell your story, someone else will. And when someone else tells your story, it won't be the story you want told."

The story they were telling about Denise was simple: she was a classic villain. She was a latter-day Cruella Deville, sneering at the offended sensibilities of the good citizens of Hampden.

She was the Grinch Who Stole Hon.

But after speaking extensively with Denise, I saw a different side of this person I'd read and heard about. I saw a genuine, deeply-wounded person who needed help. Denise hated the isolated life she was now forced to endure. And she didn't know how to navigate her way out.

We needed to change the "villain" narrative in a hurry and humanize this good person. At the same time, Denise had to become stronger and embrace the skepticism.

Our first order of business was to develop a core messaging and media plan, focusing on key points Denise would convey in answering reporters' questions.

A few examples:

Q: Why trademark the word Hon. Do you own it?

A: As in any industry around the world, each business must protect its brand and ability to operate. It is a common and sound business practice embraced by many. (Business perspective was important as Denise was merely doing what every sharp business person does, man or woman).

Q: By trademarking Hon, did you steal something from Baltimore?

A: Not at all—we are sound business stewards for the term. Our business goal is to keep the term in its rightful home: Baltimore. No one owns the rich traditions of the city—we only embrace them for a period of time before we pass the baton to the next generation. If the term is not trademarked, anyone could move to own it and take it from our city.

Q: With the negative reaction to the trademark, why don't you just give it up?

A: Cafe Hon has been in business for nearly 20 years and I plan to continue to operate here in Baltimore for years to come. If we give up legal protection of the term "Hon" for restaurant services, retail services or T-shirts, we expose the business and all that we have worked for. Again, the legal goal is solely to protect the business interest, not restrict speech or make others feel as if they cannot use the term in conversation. Others may decide to trademark the term who will not keep it in Baltimore.

The strategy was similar with the Cafe Hon website and the various digital platforms where she was being hounded. This was where the real conversation was occurring, not on the marble stoops that real Baltimore Hons still lovingly scrubbed with soap and water each weekend.

Denise had been avoiding everyone, paralyzed with uncertainty over what to do. We urged her to respond and be present, to tell her story with authenticity and meaning. We had to work on Denise's confidence and build her inner conviction—the same determination she relied on to build her business as a single mother during the previous two decades. It was there, we simply had to light the fire again.

We also needed to deal with the very aggressive, hostile and malicious group of people who were bullying Denise and wanted to see her fail at every turn. These were people who enjoyed kicking others while they were down. They basked in other people's problems.

Should Denise Whiting have made the business decision to trademark "Hon?" Maybe, maybe not. It didn't matter. It was a *business* decision that was largely misunderstood by the populace. And now it was a toxic issue ruining her business and personal life.

Clearly, she wasn't an axe murderer or criminal who preyed on the vulnerable. So did the perception that she stole the term "Hon" warrant all this backlash and behavior? Absolutely not. It was a mob mentality at its worst, people operating on the streets and social media platforms with a high degree of anonymity. Denise wasn't challenging it because she was beaten down and scared.

One of the leaders of the anti-Whiting bullies was a young man who stalked and harassed Denise, both in-person and online. He also pasted Hon stickers with a slash through them everywhere in Hampden. (This was the same charming individual who would bolt into Cafe Hon when it was packed with diners and scream.)

In my view, this type of behavior was absolutely intolerable. While he may have disagreed with Denise's business tactic, it gave him no right to break the law and try to instill fear and intimidation into her life and those around her. I convinced Denise to go to court—in fact, I went with her—to obtain a peace order and set a court date, severely restricting the man's access to her. He ended up writing a letter of apology and swore never to be around her again. To this day, he has not been a factor in her life.

My philosophy on bullying is simple: sometimes you've got to punch the bully right in the nose—at least metaphorically—so everyone gets the message that you're not going to take it anymore. In other words, this type of behavior is unacceptable and will not be tolerated. This was our figurative right cross to the bully's snout. Denise began to feel more and more confident—she had a team on her side that didn't fear confrontation.

The bottom line with bullies: start by very assertively expressing that their tactics won't be tolerated. If it continues, hold them accountable by any lawful means possible—progressive discipline, police reports, criminal court, civil court, etc. Make no apologies for criminally or civilly pursuing those who hurt others or destroy property.

I also accompanied Denise to several merchant association meetings attended by other business owners, managers and elected officials. They, too, were protesting and balking at her business posture. Again, we strongly encouraged Denise to tell her story and face the music so she could control her message at the grass-roots level, rather than letting everyone else do it for her. Denise was carefully scripted and rehearsed—this was no time for missteps.

It was uncomfortable for her. But our goal was to bring people from negative to neutral about Denise, not to make them advocates—although we would gladly take that. We needed to take the edge off the issue and restore Denise's "humanity." Denise had chosen not to attend these important meetings in the past; however, with each meeting, she grew more confident in her ability to defend her position.

In addition, we set up security details with the Baltimore Police Department to watch her and her business at HonFest. That was where the majority of activity was occurring. The threats and actions against her were becoming more aggressive. Not to sound overly dramatic, but you never knew who was going to do what to get their proverbial 15 minutes of fame and become the "community hero."

Still, we urged her to celebrate HonFest and do what she had always done, just a little more cautiously and with a few more plainclothes police officers near her. Bullies want to see their victims change their behavior—it gives them a feeling of power and control. We were determined not to let that happen.

If you're strong and exhibiting professional behavior, you send the clear message that you won't be intimidated. This deprives bullies of their self-anointed heroism and takes away their control.

Within weeks of working with Denise, I saw her gradually becoming physically and mentally stronger, a much more confident person, and a more focused and determined leader. She was becoming resilient again.

I knew she was that under normal circumstances. After all, she had survived in a cutthroat business for many years. I just happened to become part of her life at her lowest point and was grateful to have the opportunity to gain her trust while aligning her mind, body and spirit so she could run her business and lead her life.

During our engagement with Denise, she was contacted by "Kitchen Nightmares." This was the FOX network reality television show starring chef Gordon Ramsay that purports to revitalize troubled restaurants.

I talked to Denise about whether or not it was smart to have Cafe

Hon featured on the show, encouraging her to take advantage of the national opportunity on many fronts. Ultimately, she decided it was a way to put the whole trademarking "Hon" issue behind her.

"If nobody will listen to me when I say I'm sorry," she said, "maybe they'll listen when I do it on national television."

Ramsay and his crew arrived that November. The chef immediately set about jazzing-up what he saw as Cafe Hon's ho-hum menu and décor. He also helped tamp down the increasing tension developing between a harried Denise and her staff, which, understandably at the time, felt both mistreated and ignored by their besieged boss. What we learned by working with Denise was that her team wanted to be heard and validated. They loved the brand, but had very real concerns about their futures.

Ramsay, like me, seemed equally concerned about the dreadful PR hit Denise continued to take within the community.

"There was a level of hatred that was almost untouchable," Ramsay told the media. "I've never known a restaurant to have such a huge issue."

I had been encouraging Denise for weeks to consider relinquishing the trademark rights to "Hon," thinking it was not worth all the pushback she was getting from all sides. Ultimately, I felt Denise would "win" in the court of law, but lose in the court of public opinion as the community continued rendering verdict after personal verdict, week after week. And if she lost in the court of public opinion, who cared about the court of civil law—there would be no business!

In the days that "Kitchen Nightmares" filmed at her restaurant—and after speaking with Gordon Ramsay—Denise arrived at a similar epiphany. So one morning, with Ramsay in tow and the FOX cameras rolling, she went on a local morning radio program to finally announce the surrender of her "Hon" trademark.

"I am sorry for the animosity and the hatred and everything that trade-marking a word has done," Whiting told listeners, sounding almost numb. ". . . (It) has not only almost killed me, but it has just about killed the business."

After almost a year of turmoil and controversy, Denise Whiting's long ordeal was finally over. By the time she and Ramsay held a press conference later that day at the sparkling, renovated Cafe Hon, with its leopard-skin banquettes and bold wall decorations, she sounded both relieved and hopeful for the first time in months.

"I had the first good night's sleep I had in a year," she said, smiling wanly for the cameras, a villain in Hampden no more.

KEY TAKEAWAYS

1. **Earn the trust of your client, quickly.** When first inter-acting with a person embroiled in crisis, understand they are very fragile and must be emotionally supported. They don't know whom to trust and are searching for hope in an otherwise hopeless circumstance; at least that's how it seems to them.

2. **Be painfully honest and direct.** What people in crisis need is someone who will not sugar-coat the problem, but clearly explain the navigational fix. Once a person in crisis understands the situation with clarity, the rebuilding pro-cess can begin. Earn the trust of those who depend on you by operating with absolute precision and clarity. There is no better trust builder than truth.

3. **Be available all the time, at any hour.** Those feeling the pain of crisis will want to talk when they feel lonely or vul-nerable—many times, this will be early morning or late at night. It is imperative you be there for them—otherwise, you will quickly become irrelevant and lose the trust you so diligently worked to gain.

4. **Bullies don't get a free pass—hold them accountable.** Make bullies retreat to their corner of the world. Make no apologies for holding others accountable. People who are broken from crisis depend on you, as a crisis leader,

to fight for them because they can't fight for, or protect themselves, any longer. Sadly, many in this world prey on those who are down for personal gain—notoriety, financial, relational and otherwise. Understand the unique motivations of the bully and hit him or her where they are most vulnerable. What many don't understand is that court documents and proceedings in most cases are public record. Should the bully find himself or herself in court, quite often a spouse, employer or other meaningful person or entity will discover the bully's transgressions. Often, the thought of "silver bracelets" has a way of deterring even the most brazen bullies, who only seem to have a backbone when their friends are cheering them on. In the most severe cases, when there may be a mental health issue at play, use every lawful means necessary to protect yourself and your business. Most bullies retreat when they realize the proverbial "kid they steal lunch money from" knows how to fight back, because you, as a crisis leader, are now in their corner.

5. **Control your message.** Like many in difficult situations, Denise became overwhelmed and didn't know how to manage the court of public opinion, traditionally or digitally. As a result, all of the "haters" spoke for and about her, unchallenged. And when the drumbeat of negativity or rumor persists without balance, the fictions become fact. It is imperative to quickly control your message from the onset of any crisis. In this digital world, anyone can broadcast an opinion quickly, with conviction. You must do the same, with credibility and balance!

3

When You're the 8-Point Buck

Ed Norris' fall from grace was as swift and stunning as any in recent memory.

The worst moment, he told me, came in the middle of his six-month sentence in federal prison, as he lay on the floor of a sweltering cell in Atlanta he shared with two other inmates.

"I'm wearing pants that are too small, a shirt that's five sizes too big, I had two different colored sneakers on and I'm holding a newspaper rolled up in tape against the door with my feet to keep the rats out," he recalled.

"Two guys in the bunk are smoking meth or whatever. I started to laugh uncontrollably. I'm thinking: *I can't believe a year ago I was the Colonel of the Maryland State Police! How the fuck did they ever get away with this?*"

Ed was hardly the first public servant to be unceremoniously drummed from office. But the story of how Maryland's top crime fighter landed behind bars made international headlines, pegged as yet another cautionary tale of a powerful figure brought down by greed and a lavish taste for the good life.

Over drinks and dinner at a Baltimore chop house one evening, he told me his story:

Built along the lines of a chimney, with a prizefighter's mug and an inherent love for chasing bad guys, Ed Norris seemed born to be a cop.

He was the son of a New York City patrolman and a rising star in the NYPD when then-Mayor Martin O'Malley lured him to Baltimore in 2000 to be deputy police commissioner.

Within months, he had ascended to commissioner, eager to help the young mayor fulfill his campaign pledge to get crime under control. Norris vowed to bring Baltimore's infamous murder count under 300 for the first time in more than 10 years, improve the sagging morale of the 3,200-member police force, and root out corrupt cops.

He quickly backed up the brash talk.

Emerging as a larger-than-life figure, he swaggered around town in his crisp uniform, black leather jacket and shades, head shaved smooth as a cue-ball. Tales of the new commissioner leaping from his cruiser to personally slap the handcuffs on drug dealers abounded. So did stories of his epic carousing at upscale bars and restaurants.

He shook up the department, changing beats and firing senior officers. He made cops used to day shifts work nights, because that was when the criminals worked. He made going after dangerous fugitives a priority. He was a cop's cop.

He seemed to show up after every police shooting. If the shooting was justified, he'd huddle with the shaken cop and say, "Good job," letting him know the new commish had his back.

When the media arrived, Ed Norris would step in front of the TV cameras and say: "This officer did what he was sworn to do. We should all be proud of him."

His fellow cops loved him. How could they not? Criminals feared him. He fought with the City Council and ticked off some in the community with his tough tactics, but also developed a reputation with others as a New York hothead and showboat.

But for many in Baltimore—the city O'Malley called the most violent and addicted in the country—Ed Norris was a genuine civic hero.

Crime fell dramatically. So did the homicide count. The papers took to calling the young mayor and his top cop "Batman and Robin." For the first time in years, there was a sense the city was a better, safer place for its citizens.

"I was the greatest thing since Cal Ripken, Jr.," he laughed.

A couple of years later, it all began to unravel.

It started with seemingly innocuous questions about an off-the-books expense account.

The Baltimore Sun reported that Norris used the little-known supplemental fund for expensive dinners at steak houses, weekends at the opulent W Hotel in Manhattan, Orioles tickets and assorted souvenirs.

"They started beating my brains in with this," Norris recalled. "They tried to misrepresent this as taxpayer money. It wasn't. It was a fund that originated in pre-Depression Baltimore that was put together by police for widows and orphans.

"It was the commissioners' discretionary fund. They could use it any way they wanted, with no oversight."

Police commissioners had used the fund for generations. Norris insisted to everyone that he did nothing wrong.

The pricey steak dinners? Not so pricey when you consider he brought along four staff members, he said. One New York trip was to attend a funeral. He paid for the O's tickets himself. The souvenirs were inexpensive trinkets he'd give to out-of-town visitors as a good-will gesture. Most of the money that was spent—some $179,000—was determined to have gone toward legitimate departmental expenses. But some $20,000 was red-flagged. Norris agreed to pay back the money he'd spent on alleged "personal items."

Still, the allegations and intense scrutiny were wearing on him. So was the job itself. At a meeting with Gov. Robert L. Ehrlich to see how the state police could help the city, Norris says Ehrlich popped the question: "How would you like to be the state police superintendent?"

Norris was immediately intrigued.

"A lot of stuff was going down in Baltimore," he told me. "Racial politics, everything else…I was under tremendous stress there. Because we took such an aggressive crime stance, I buried seven cops in three years. That takes a toll on you personally.

"It was very hard for me. I never slept. I tried to appear like I was everywhere. I'd go home at 8 at night and be back out at 2 in the morning. I was exhausted. This was a chance to not be exhausted."

In December of 2002, Norris agreed to head the Maryland State Police. O'Malley was upset, Norris says, but sent him a beautiful framed photo of Ulysses S. Grant as a going-away gift.

This was an inside joke. When crime in Baltimore was down, the mayor would refer to Norris as General Grant, the Civil War hero for the Union. When crime spiked, Norris became Gen. George B. McClellan, whom President Abraham Lincoln replaced for being ineffective.

Critics immediately accused Norris of abandoning the city. Things soon got worse for the swashbuckling new state police boss. Weeks later, federal prosecutors began their own investigation of his tenure in Baltimore.

The U.S. Attorney's office seized files from police headquarters as evidence. Now the feeling around Ed Norris was that of a gathering storm, one that could sweep in and batter him at any moment. Was this a politically-motivated investigation for leaving Baltimore after only a few years? Some said so.

"It was tremendous pressure," he said. "I would collapse in my office sometimes. I had to catch my breath. I couldn't function some days. I'd walk out of a meeting and I'd smile and shake hands. Then I'd go into my office and almost fall down. My knees would buckle.

"Keep in mind, as I'm doing this, I'm trying to run a police department, trying to keep my family intact. And every media member in Baltimore who has my number…is calling and saying: 'I hear there's a sealed indictment coming on Friday.'"

Norris would lose it during those conversations.

"DO YOU THINK I KNOW?!" he'd yell at reporters. "DO YOU REALLY FUCKING THINK THEY'D TELL ME FIRST?"

He learned that the feds had gone through his bank records and visited his parents' house in Brooklyn. Norris had borrowed $9,000 from his father when he'd bought his house in Baltimore. His father had signed the money off as a gift.

But prosecutors had found a check in Norris' records that indicated he'd paid his dad back. So now the gift was being considered a loan.

"'That's the headshot,'" Norris says a high-powered attorney told him. "'They're going to pepper the indictment with things you didn't do. They're going to indict you for bank fraud and mortgage fraud, and they're going to force a plea because they have you on that.'"

In a moment of despair, Norris asked Ehrlich: "Why are they doing this to me?"

Norris says the answer was succinct.

"You're the 8-point buck in the state," the governor replied. "Who else are they gonna do this to?"

The indictment was announced in December of 2003. In addition to charges of misusing some $20,000 and lying on a mortgage loan application, it contained lurid details of extra-marital encounters.

There was other stuff he could explain away, like more than $5,000 used to entertain deserving officers and colleagues at Orioles games. He was charged with buying boots for personal use—he said they were combat boots for work. Same thing with a knife that was listed. Interestingly, the final restitution request for gifts in Norris' case was a whopping $100!

Norris resigned as state police superintendent the day the indictment was announced. His instinct, he told everyone, was to fight the charges. But on a chilly March morning in 2004, he showed up at U.S. District Court in Baltimore. Standing grim-faced before a judge, he pleaded guilty to conspiring to misuse money from the supplemental account and lying on tax returns.

"He made the decision," his lawyer explained outside the courthouse, "that a long, drawn-out trial would bring too much pain to his family, his friends and the city of Baltimore."

By this point, of course, his loved ones were already in plenty of pain.

The day after the indictments were handed down, Norris's wife, Kathryn Norris, was stopped at an intersection in her car. Suddenly someone lunged at her, holding up the front page of *The Sun* that showed a photo of her husband and the headline: "Chief Lies, Cheats, Steals."

Those were the comments Maryland U.S. Attorney Thomas DiBiagio had made to reporters one day earlier—the same day that Norris' father, the proud former New York cop, had listened to the charges being read in court and became so distraught he had to leave.

Norris was sentenced to six months in prison, followed by six months of house arrest and community service.

In the weeks that followed, he was overwhelmed with feelings of fear, anger and shame. The thought of going to prison terrified him—everyone knew that doing time as an ex-cop could be its own form of hell.

He thought about suicide.

"I sat in Robert E. Lee Park with my gun," he said, tearing up at the memory.

What kept him from pulling the trigger? The thought of his son, Jack, then 5, living without a dad.

From then on, he did everything he could to keep his mind off what lay ahead.

"I went into husband-father mode," he said. "I kept myself extremely busy doing things to at least keep the family intact. I also bought toys for every week I'd be away. I put them in envelopes with a card. And my wife gave one to my kid every week, which she said I had mailed."

Soon after the indictments, he moved his family to Tampa.

Baltimore was too hot, in the figurative sense. Too uncomfortable. Too many bad memories. He was done with the city. So was his wife.

"We've got to get the fuck out of here," Kathryn Norris kept saying.

In some ways, the last few days of freedom were the hardest. One night, he sat with Jack watching a Spiderman/Daredevil animated series on TV.

"Why is Spiderman in jail?" the boy asked suddenly, pointing at the screen.

Norris' thoughts were a million miles away. He tried to re-focus. *What?! Spiderman's in the slammer?* How do you answer that one?

"Well, Jack," Norris said finally, "sometimes good people get put away by bad people."

The day before he was due to report to the federal prison camp at Eglin Air Force Base in the Florida Panhandle, a minimum-security facility, two old friends, former New York City detectives, flew down to Tampa.

"I wouldn't let my wife or my dad drive me to prison," Norris explained.

Instead, he and his buddies took off in a rented car. They drove through the Panhandle intent on raising hell one last time.

"Remember the Jack Nicholson movie 'The Last Detail?'" Norris said, referring to the 1973 film about two Navy men ordered to bring a young sailor to prison, but who decide to show the kid a good time first. "We went to a strip club, we had steak, we got drunk."

The next morning at 10, brutally hung over, Norris was banging on his buddies' motel-room doors shouting: "Get up! The faster I'm in prison, the faster I get out! So let's get this done!"

At the prison gates, Norris had one last request.

"Just fucking leave," he said. "Don't look at me. Just drive away. I'll see you when I get out."

His buddies left and didn't utter a word to one another for more than an hour on the car ride back. They, too, were emotionally spent and couldn't believe they had just dropped one of the best cops they knew at a prison gate.

Prison life was harsh, but not as bad as he had feared.

After processing, which included a strip search, the issuing of prison clothes, a physical and a session with a psychiatrist, Norris was assigned to a cell with six bunks. Scared of introducing himself as a former cop, he says he made up a "stupid story" about who he was and why he'd been incarcerated.

An inmate took him aside and said: "Look, we know who you are. We get newspapers in here. And people talk. Don't worry. You're fine."

The inmate turned out to be Martin Grass, the disgraced former CEO of Rite Aid. Grass was doing an eight-year sentence for directing an accounting fraud. He and Norris would become friends. Three other inmates in the cell were drug dealers. The fourth was a former judge from New Orleans.

Norris let everyone else think he was a meth dealer. He soon settled into the mind-numbing, soul-crushing routine that is life behind bars.

He got a job in the kitchen. He was relieved to find that rape happened infrequently, since there was plenty of sex to go around if an inmate wanted it. He learned the various rituals you needed to learn to get by. One involved knocking on the table before rising after a meal, a signal that you weren't getting up to stick a knife in someone's back.

"I worked out, lost 40 pounds, read 70 books," he said. "…I wrote letters every day, got a ton of mail and that keeps you going. I set goals every day. Mine were to get fit, breathe and prepare for what's coming next."

In prison, he learned that his nemesis, DiBiagio, the U.S. Attorney who had brought charges against him, had "resigned" amid allegations that he had ordered subordinates to produce other "front-page" indictments. Still, the news did little to cheer Ed Norris at the time. Prison is a place where your emotions shut down. Joy is hard to come by.

After hurricanes hit the Panhandle, he was transferred to a prison in Yazoo City, Miss., then to the federal camp in Atlanta. The inmates he'd become friendly with promised Norris they wouldn't divulge his identity.

But on the day of his release, news trucks descended on the prison, waiting for him to come out of the gates.

Other prisoners watched the TV cameras setting up, stared at him and asked: "Who the fuck *are* you?"

Good question. Even Ed Norris didn't know anymore.

He was 45, a convicted felon. What would he do now? He needed a job. He was on home detention with an ankle bracelet, able to leave home only for work, church and the gym. But who would hire him?

Nevertheless, he started looking. Every day. But every job application asked: "Have you ever been convicted of a crime?" Finally, he filled-out one that didn't and got a job at a high-end perfumery at a Tampa mall.

He made $8 an hour and liked the job just fine. He says he was a valued employee.

"Then I got a call one day from the manager," he said. "Someone recognized me and called the company. So the manager said 'So sorry' and fired me. I said 'You want me to bring the key back?' She said no, they already changed the locks.

"So I got fired! From a minimum wage job! At the *mall!* I'd been out for three months. You wonder why people go back to their criminal behavior? They have to get money somehow."

A Tampa newspaper reporter got wind of Norris' story and stopped by his house to see if he'd talk about his situation.

It was a bad day to drop by.

"I can't wrap my brain around it," he told her. "I'm sitting in the smoldering wreck that is my life."

But little by little, the clouds began to lift.

In August of 2005, he got a call from a radio station in Baltimore. How would he like to do an hourly talk show every day from his

Tampa home?

He was still immensely popular in Charm City. The station had taken a poll of listeners, asking: "Would you want Ed Norris back as police commissioner?" Ninety percent of the callers said yes. Evidently, they felt Ed Norris had made Baltimore safer. He had delivered on his promise to reduce crime.

So he accepted the radio gig. When a judge decreed that Norris had to perform his community service in Baltimore, he flew north, slept in a friend's basement and continued to do the show, returning home on weekends to see his family.

With his service requirements fulfilled a year later, he asked the station for a long-term contract. Otherwise, he told them, I'm moving back to Florida with my family. The station gave him what he wanted and he moved his family to the Baltimore metropolitan area.

Pretty soon, Ed Norris was getting great ratings, making six figures and reclaiming his old celebrity status, this time via the airwaves. He was even asked by David Simon to play a detective known as Edward Norris on the hit HBO series, "The Wire."

More than ten years later, he still works in radio as the co-host of the top-rated sports-talk "Norris and Davis Show" on 105.7 The Fan.

But as dessert and after-dinner drinks are served at the chophouse, Ed Norris frowns when I ask him how life is going these days.

"Am I content? No," he says. "I still didn't do anything wrong. It's nice that I make more money than I did as police commissioner. I have an easy job. I have a nicer car…People are always telling me 'You're doing great!' (But) I'm not a crook. And I have to live with this. And I'm out of a profession that I was the best at."

"I tell people: 'That's what I was meant to do.' I was really good at that. If your mother was the victim of a crime, you'd want me to have the case.'"

KEY TAKEAWAYS

1. **Keep your family intact.** Crisis causes tremendous

amounts of short- and long-term strain and there are many instances when people in crisis have a difficult time managing themselves, much less others around them. However, when it comes down to it, your family is really all you have—they are the people that love you unconditionally. Most have heard that you "hurt the ones you love the most." Flip the paradigm and do everything in your power to maintain your family structure. Families are generally the unintended victims and everything must be done to protect them from the people or circumstances that threaten your physical and emotional well-being.

2. **Preserve your own life.** In virtually every high-profile crisis case I've been a part of, clients have said that the thought of suicide entered their mind, particularly when there is intense media scrutiny. The rationale? Clients felt as if there was simply no way out. They were disgraced, humiliated, embarrassed and beaten down—they had no fight and lost their will to live. These were generally good-hearted people who reached a breaking point—they felt they had more value dead than alive. Their self-esteem was destroyed and they wanted the pain to simply go away. There are so many resources to help one get through life's most difficult times. And, to a person, everyone I've interacted with who thought of suicide is glad they didn't do it. Sadly, when someone takes his or her own life, the pain is passed on to those who love them. If you can make it through the rough patch by leaning forward, life will get better.

3. **Know your numbers, above and below the line.** We've all heard the saying that money is the root of all evil. Based on my experience, money that is mismanaged wittingly or unwittingly triggers long-term crisis. As a newly-appointed chief executive, never completely trust what others

are telling you, particularly when it comes to the financial side of the shop. While it was very easy to rely on the fiscal advice Norris was given about the discretionary fund, he admits he should have been more diligent and less accepting of embracing the "that's the way we've always done it" mindset. Thoroughly scrub each budget you are accountable for, particularly as a new executive. Trust but verify!

4. **Lead from the front.** Norris talks frequently about leading from the front and not asking anyone who works for you to do anything you wouldn't do yourself. Whether Norris was chasing an armed suspect down a dark alley or testifying before combative community members or legislators, the men and women in blue knew he had their back and was acting in their best interest. Be the example and those that are loyal and motivated will operate within that shadow. Real results are driven by leaders who operate in the trenches.

KEY CONCEPT

Eddie Haskell
vs. the Eagle Scout

Imagine two 10 year-old boys playing in the neighborhood they grew up in. The first boy, we'll call him Tim, is running around, picking up rocks and throwing them. One of the rocks happens to go through his neighbor's window. Very scared, Tim looks around, sees no one, then runs in the back door of his home and directly up to his room. There, he quickly shuts the door, looks out the window to ensure he wasn't seen, then begins playing video games. (I would say read a book, but this is 2016).

What Tim didn't realize was that an 80-year-old woman, we'll call her Mrs. Cindy, was sitting by her window (as she does every day) and saw Tim throw the rock that broke his neighbor's window. Mrs. Cindy can't help but call the "victimized" neighbor, Mr. Brendan, to let him know what happened. One thing leads to another, Tim's parents get called and before you know it, Tim is crying in front of Mr. Brendan, admitting his guilt and paying restitution. Tim is talked about all over town—he now has the Eddie Haskell reputation!

The second boy, we'll call him Garrett, does the exact same thing— he throws a rock through a neighbor's window. Although scared, upset and crying, he goes home and tells his Mom and Dad what happened. Well, Garrett ends up crying in front of Mr. Brendan as well. However, because he was proactive and apologetic, Mr. Brendan lets him off the hook, emotionally and financially. In fact, because he was honest and forthright, Garrett's personal equity goes through the roof! Now, Mr. Brendan is telling everyone about his experience with Garrett and what a fine young man he his. Garrett earned the "Eagle Scout Reputation."

This very basic character comparison speaks volumes about how leaders today handle crises, particularly issues that cause personal embarrassment. So many are afraid to raise their hand and take personal responsibility. When Steve Harvey royally screwed up and announced the wrong winner in the 2015 Miss Universe pageant, he didn't blame others or do the "Potomac two-step." He immediately apologized and did the best he could under a very public, humiliating circumstance.

Yes, everyone beat the living stew out of him for a few days, particularly on Twitter. But once the storm passed, most people understood that he had simply screwed up. Handled any differently, Harvey would have had even more explaining to do.

4

While Baltimore Burned, a City Cried Out for Leadership

The afternoon and evening of April 27, 2015 will stay with me forever.

Following the funeral of a 25-year-old African-American man named Freddie Gray who had died under questionable circumstances in police custody, Baltimore erupted in a terrifying spate of rioting and looting that seemed to paralyze the city's top officials with fear and indecision—a condition I observed first-hand for days.

As a crisis leadership expert and former chief spokesperson for the Baltimore Police Department, I'm often asked by the local and national media to comment on public safety and leadership issues. So as rioting spread across the city, with crowds of angry young people gathering to pelt police with rocks and bottles, and as dozens of stores and businesses were sacked and destroyed, I was not surprised to get a call from CNN.

A producer asked: Could I appear live on Don Lemon's show outside City Hall from 10 p.m. to 1 a.m.? Images of burning buildings and looted stores were already being broadcast around the world. Coming after days of mostly peaceful demonstrations, the unrest was now alternately riveting and horrifying the nation just eight months after the violent protests over police brutality in Ferguson, Mo.

After thinking about whether or not I wanted to get caught up in the mix, I told the producer I'd be at the interview site, in front of Baltimore's City Hall. I felt I had a perspective to lend that many did not, given my experience in Baltimore's police force and understanding of the city. In fact, I've interviewed with CNN, FOX, MSNBC, BBC, VOA and a host of other national and international news networks and cable outlets throughout my career, so I understood the importance of lending credible insight in a balanced manner.

I knew many would use this media platform as a chance to advance an agenda or "sound off" about whatever irked them during this emotional time. I felt an obligation to speak about Baltimore and on the very important, volatile issue of police brutality.

Driving into the city from my home that night was a surreal experience.

Before I reached I-395, the ribbon of highway that curls around the outskirts of Baltimore before spilling out downtown, I could see the fires burning in the distance.

The smell of smoke hung heavy in the air. The wail of sirens was everywhere. Each news report on the radio seemed to confirm that things were growing increasingly out of control, and that the police were completely overwhelmed by the chaos in the streets.

For the first time in my career, I had actually brought a licensed, armed person with me to an interview for personal protection. I felt better having Frank Barile, who heads Fallston Group's safety and security vertical, watching my back.

Frank is a former highly-decorated Baltimore County police officer and SWAT team member—a weapons and tactical expert. The unrest was clearly growing in intensity, and my fear was that we could come upon a large group of rioters who might decide to make us their next target.

There was no question that Freddie Gray's death had become a rallying point for much of West Baltimore and its impoverished residents. So many were frustrated with the historical conditions in which they were forced to live, with the joblessness, the lack of transportation, the lack of opportunity, no education and, quite frankly, with the lack of hope.

These are all extremely important social issues that must continue to be addressed. Baltimore was now a city of the "have's" and "have not's." It can be a recipe for disaster when the poorest are just blocks away from the most privileged, as we've seen in many American cities.

The main question now was: what would city leadership—particularly Mayor Stephanie Rawlings-Blake and Police Commissioner Anthony Batts—do to quell the unrest and get the city back under control?

The answer, sadly, turned out to be: not nearly enough. Certainly not in the critical first hours, when the violence escalated alarmingly and city officials seemed nowhere to be found.

As I stood outside City Hall being interviewed about the rapidly deteriorating conditions, about Freddie Gray's arrest and police department policy on prisoner transport and use of force, the questions I heard over and over again from media members and citizens were: "Where's the mayor? How come we haven't heard from her yet?"

The city was clamoring for leadership, for direction. City officials had allegedly been trying to get in touch with the mayor all afternoon, going so far as to send her frantic emails asking: "WHAT ARE YOU DOING?"

How were the police being deployed? Were they arresting rioters or merely containing them? Would a state of emergency be declared and the National Guard called in? Were other police agencies on the way to help an under-resourced department?

No one knew. And during such a critical time, when you're the mayor of a big city, you have to balance your time between managing the crisis and being the face of the city. During life's most critical times, people need direction. In fact, research shows that people would rather follow someone who made a wrong decision than no decision at all.

Not until more than five hours after the unrest started, after some 20 police officers had been injured, over a dozen buildings torched and dozens more vandalized, along with hundreds of cars damaged or destroyed, would Baltimore's mayor hold a press conference.

In a strangely subdued voice, she faced the TV cameras and said: "What we see tonight going on in our city is very disturbing."

She said the National Guard would be deployed to secure the peace as soon as possible. (Rumors had been flying for hours that Maryland's Republican governor, Larry Hogan, had been waiting to hear from the Democratic mayor about activating a state of emergency.)

She said a nighttime curfew would be imposed on the city. "We will be holding people accountable," she said.

And she defended her ill-chosen remarks of two days earlier, when she'd told reporters: "While we tried to make sure that (those protesting the police treatment of Freddie Gray) were protected from the cars and the other things that were going on, we also gave those who wished to destroy space to do that as well."

"I did not say we were being passive (about) it," she said now, appearing agitated and insisting her words had been mischaracterized by the media.

It was a disastrous performance. For many, it confirmed the obvious: at a time when her city needed firm leadership the most, Stephanie Rawlings-Blake had seemingly been asleep at the switch or receiving incredibly horrible advice, neither of which are acceptable.

As it happened, a few hours after her press conference, just as I finished another interview on Don Lemon's show, the mayor and Gov. Hogan suddenly appeared on the CNN set. Both looked tense and exhausted. I knew this was not a time for politics, but a time for a joint, reassuring public safety message.

As I finished a live shot, I took a step back off set and exchanged a brief "How are you doing?" with the mayor. The mayor had changed out of the business-like outfit she'd worn earlier into jeans and a three-quarter length gray puffer coat. It was her ready-to-hit-the-streets look, her take-charge look. But she hardly seemed more energized.

I stood literally two feet behind the mayor and governor as they spoke live. Yet this interview did little to change the impression that the mayor had been slow to act, and that her indecisiveness had made a difficult situation even worse.

Again, she haltingly defended her remarks about giving protestors space to destroy. "What I said very clearly was...when you facilitate space for people to be heard, that space was exploited by those who meant to do harm to our city." Lemon was unrelenting as he grilled her.

Hogan offered what seemed to be tepid praise for the response of Ms. Rawlings-Blake and city officials to the riots, saying: "They've had this under control."

But then he seemed to take a subtle jab at the Democratic mayor by adding: "It escalated to the point this evening, or late this afternoon, where it was out of control. And when the mayor called and asked us to declare a state of emergency, we were ready and prepared and we did so immediately."

Moments later, after Lemon continued to press both officials about the lack of leadership and the late response to the violence in the streets, the interview came to an abrupt close as both officials walked off the live shot.

Don Lemon turned to me, made a face and said: "That was extremely awkward."

I had to agree. My impression of their remarks was that there seemed to be little solidarity between Rawlings-Blake and Hogan, and that they were not on the same page in terms of strategy and tactics moving forward.

As her handlers and security personnel guided her to a waiting SUV, an even more pressing thought occurred to me: this was likely the beginning of the end for Stephanie Rawlings-Blake's tenure as

Baltimore's mayor.

Knowing what I know about crisis leadership—being a student
of it and being in the business—I knew this: as Baltimore waited for
direction from the highest local official, and continued to wait for
hours on end, the mayor's reputational equity was dwindling fast.

When thrust into a crisis situation, citizens want to sense optimism in their leader, and I don't mean optimism in a Pollyanna-ish
way. Citizens want to know who is in charge. They want to have a
sense of confidence and belief that the leader is going to harness every
resource possible to bring the crisis to stability. Leaders must be ready
to meet the moment.

In fairness, this—the riots—was something Stephanie Rawlings-
Blake had never handled before. And on the heels of what had happened in Ferguson, and how quickly events there had spiraled out of
control, she had probably taken an "oh-my-God, I-hope-this-goes-
away" approach instead of taking the bull by the horns, being direc-
tional and letting people know what the consequences of their actions
would be. She may have done this operationally through experienced
experts, but the gap in communicating this stance publicly was larger
than the Grand Canyon.

The mayor might have also been afraid that she would appear
weak or over-reactive if she called for the state to send in the National
Guard when the riots first started. The business of politics may have
clouded her judgment, too. Hogan, the Republican governor, was
thought by many of the city's leaders to have a tin ear when it came to
the many urban ills that plagued Baltimore.

But this was a time for the mayor to put her ego aside and not
view the situation through a political lens. This was the time to put
party aside. This was the time to gain control of the riots and provide
stability to citizens.

Stephanie Rawlings-Blake did none of those things. She allowed
the leadership moment of a lifetime to pass her by.

In my view, it was the faith-based community that actually

stepped up and made a difference in restoring calm to the city. While the insertion of Maryland's resources, via the Army National Guard and Maryland State Police, and an implemented curfew, created a sense of calm on the streets, community-based leaders ultimately rose to the occasion.

It was Baltimore church leaders, as well as older citizens, who took to the streets to counsel the mostly young people involved in the unrest: "Whoa, whoa, whoa! Wait a minute! There's a better way! You're destroying our homes! You're destroying our city! You're giving us a bad name!"

I heard this and a variation of these phrases repeated during the week of the unrest.

One thing was certain, though: the mayor's quote about giving protestors space to destroy would haunt her for many months.

I firmly believe in holding people accountable. That's what a good leader does. If you throw a rock, bottle or brick, destroy property or hurt someone, you must be held accountable. You don't get a free pass. And what I heard from the mayor's remarks was that the city and its resources would do everything possible to give people room to act out, but not hold them accountable for destruction. Regardless of intent, we all know the most important message is the message received.

When you destroy someone's home or business, you potentially destroy their lives. People would rather get hit in the head with a brick and recover from that than have their home or business destroyed. And the long-term damage from such ruinous riots—the inability for small businesses to recover, the fear people now have about moving to a city and starting a business there—does incalculable damage to the city's image.

All told, the destruction was estimated at $9 million for about 285 businesses damaged, according to the Small Business Administration (SBA.) Nearly 150 vehicle fires and more than 60 structure fires were also reported.

As a progressive big-city mayor from a prominent political family,

Stephanie Rawlings-Blake had been a rising star in Democratic circles. But in the end, the damage inflicted on the mayor's political fortunes by the unrest would prove too much to overcome. I felt that night she wouldn't survive—it was too much of a political hit.

And it was.

On the morning of Sept. 11, 2015, the following story suddenly appeared on *The New York Times* website:

"BALTIMORE—Mayor Stephanie Rawlings-Blake, who has come under withering criticism since riots tore through this city in April, announced Friday that she would not seek re-election next year, saying she wanted to focus "on the city's future, and not my own" as Baltimore prepared for the racially-charged trials of six police officers in the death of a 25-year-old black man, Freddie Gray...."

KEY TAKEAWAYS

1. **Seize the leadership moment.** I coach my clients all of the time, and attempt to get them to quickly understand, that short-term adversity can be long-term advantage, if you are able to meet the moment with impact. Know that crisis is going to happen—embrace and seize the moment. Look for ways to make you or your company bigger, faster and stronger than you were before. Everyone makes mistakes, people trust those who handle crisis with the honesty and dignity it deserves. And in a city that in 2015 recorded the highest homicide rate (per capita) in its history, there had never been a time when strong leadership was needed more—at every level.

2. **Embrace the Resilient Moment Communications Model.** I believe the underpinning of success is the ability to communicate effectively, even in dire, unexpected circumstances. I am a big advocate of Dr. George Everly, Jr., Ph.D., one of the founding fathers of the modern era of stress management. He has been a pioneer in developing programs designed to

foster human resilience in the wake of crises, disasters and psychological trauma. I've had the good fortune of working and teaching with Dr. Everly as a core faculty member of the Resiliency Sciences Institute, International. Dr. Everly's Resilient Moment Communications model hits the nail on the head. The bottom line is this: if you answer the following questions during issues of sensitivity, adversity or crisis, you will have answered the key questions people have during life's most critical times:

What happened?

What caused it?

What are the effects—realized and anticipated?

What is being done about it?

What needs to be done in the future?

If Mayor Stephanie Rawlings Blake would have credibly and comprehensively answered these questions when she faced the world on CNN that fateful evening in Baltimore, it may have propelled vs. derailed her career.

3. **Don't retreat to the foxhole.** I've often said that our nation's military and first responders are comprised of ordinary people who are thrust into extraordinary circumstances. It is where heroes emerge and true character is revealed. Anyone can lead during prosperous times, when all is going well. However, incredible leaders emerge when the chips are down and there is seemingly no way out. I learned some really valuable leadership lessons from my father, who was an Airborne Ranger, and my mother, who was a career nursing manager, first serving her country as a nurse in Vietnam. The one lesson that has always remained with me is the power of presence. The ability to look someone in the eye with empathy and compassion during adversity is critical. In simple terms, step on or step out—lead, follow or get out of the way. You must ensure that you and

your clients are ready to meet the moment, at any cost, no matter how uncomfortable. Remember, certain life occurrences will happen whether you are there or not. You have the ability to make an immediate and valuable difference in people's lives. Make it happen with integrity, transparency and decisiveness—be ready to meet the moment!

4. **Reframe your remarks, if misunderstood.** Every single person I know has misspoken or has not articulated a point in the most optimal manner. Knowing the "space to destroy" remark was gaining a lot of negative momentum, the mayor should have gotten the media on track with a "reframing" of the remark vs. any denials or debate about its intent. I truly don't think the mayor is customarily inconsiderate or incompetent; in fact, during the times I've briefly interacted with her, she was very professional. However, this incident caused her to react with visible disgust and resentment toward those delivering her message—the news media. Remember, the media is the communications conduit with editorial control in most settings, not the ultimate consumer of information.

5

Active Shooter:
Scourge of the Modern Age

Monday, April 16, 2007, dawned cold, snowy and blustery on the campus of Virginia Tech in the rolling hills of Blacksburg, Virginia. It was the sort of morning that might cause many college students to glance out the window, shudder and go back to bed.

Shortly before 9 a.m., Colin Goddard, a 21-year-old senior majoring in International Studies, pulled up to the parking lot of Norris Hall in his car. With him was a friend named Kristina Anderson. The two were headed for an Intermediate French class.

For a moment, they discussed whether to blow off class and go out for breakfast. But ultimately, class won out. And with that seemingly benign decision, Goddard and Anderson would soon find themselves in the midst of the deadliest shooting rampage in U.S. history.

There were 17 people in the French class that day, including the teacher, Jocelyn Couture-Nowak, 49, from Montreal, Canada. Goddard and Anderson took their seats in the back of the small room.

Halfway through the class, another student, Rachael Hill, came in. She whispered that there had been a shooting in her dorm earlier in the morning and that the building had been on lockdown, which was why she was late for class.

Goddard and Anderson expressed surprise at the news. They hadn't heard about a shooting, but they assumed that was because they both lived off campus. And they thought that if Rachael had been allowed to leave the dorm, the situation was now under control.

(In fact, as they would learn later, two students had been killed in the shooting, which had occurred at 7:15 a.m. And although the school had not yet gotten the word out, the gunman was still at large.)

A few minutes later, a loud banging was heard. At first, everyone assumed it was coming from construction on the building next door.

But the banging got louder. With a concerned look on her face, Couture-Nowak opened the door to investigate. Quickly, she slammed it shut and told the students to get under their desks.

"Someone call 911!" she said.

No one knew what was happening. Goddard pulled out his cell phone and dialed the emergency number. When someone answered, he blurted: "Norris Hall, Blacksburg, Virginia." But the person on the other end had no idea what he was talking about.

Instead of being connected to a local 911 number, Goddard had mistakenly been connected to the Nextel emergency line in another state.

"Norris Hall, Virginia Tech, Blacksburg, Virginia!" he said this time, adding for good measure: "America!"

By the time he was transferred to the Blacksburg police, bullets were splintering the classroom door.

Everyone jumped on the floor, overturning chair-desks in the confusion and panic. Goddard found himself positioned along a wall.

"I took one look to the front of the room," he told me, "and what I saw was a guy walking with brown desert combat boots, khaki pants, a white shirt and two holsters crossed over his shoulders.

"….My first thought was that this was a cop who'd climbed in the windows on the other side of the room and was going to help us. Then he turned down our row of desks. And I thought: this isn't who I thought it was. I kind of turned away.

"I was thinking of making a move for the windows across the room. But in retrospect I'm glad I didn't. 'Cause I probably wouldn't be here."

Seconds later, Goddard felt something slam into his left leg, around the knee. A burning sensation followed. He went numb from head to toe and smelled gunpowder.

"I realized I just got shot!" he recalled. "This is real!"

In the chaos of the next eight and a half minutes, Goddard never lost consciousness.

The gunman left the classroom, but the students could still hear gunshots close by. Goddard realized he was still on the phone with the police. The woman on the other end of the line tried to calm him down and told him officers were on their way.

Goddard told her he'd been shot.

After a few screams, an eerie quiet descended over the classroom. Goddard heard someone near him gurgling and struggling to breathe.

Then the gunman returned.

Goddard could hear him walking around the room, shooting and not saying anything. When he came back to where Goddard huddled, he fired again and shot Goddard a second time, this time in the left hip.

"I could (still) hear the woman on the phone, and she sounded so loud!" he remembered. "I didn't want (the gunman) to know that no. 1, I was alive and no. 2, that I had made contact with the police.

"So I tried to hide my body…and just go with the force of the bullet. But it pulled the phone out of my hand. It was a flip phone and fortunately it didn't shut. And it landed next to the head of a girl, Emily (Haas), who realized what it was.

"She picked it up and put it underneath her hair and she remained on the line for the duration of the incident."

The gunman left for a second time. But he was soon back. Now the students could hear the police outside the building shouting and trying to find a way in. The gunman had chained the doors together.

He had also placed a sign on them indicating that if the doors were opened, explosives would detonate.

It would later be revealed there were no explosives, but the sign served the gunman's purpose. It stopped students from leaving the building. And it prevented the police from entering.

Finally, Goddard would learn later, the police discovered a maintenance door on the side of the building and shot the lock off to gain access. Soon the students could hear them in the building, yelling and clearing the floors one classroom at a time.

But now the gunman entered Goddard's classroom for a third time.

Goddard was lying on his side. Emily was still talking to police as the terrified students nearby whispered for her to be quiet. Goddard could hear the gunman going up and down each row again.

"I could feel him close to my feet," Goddard recalled.

Then he was shot for a third time. The bullet entered under his right shoulder. The force flipped his body around. Soon he was shot a fourth time, just above his right hip.

Somehow, Goddard was still conscious and alert. He had yet to see the gunman's face, or hear anything he said. Later, another student would report hearing a deep, maniacal laugh from the shooter.

But now the room was quiet again.

"I thought it meant he was getting prepared to engage the police," Goddard said.

By now, the SWAT team had reached the classroom. But the team couldn't open the door. The reason became evident: two bodies were blocking it. There was the last sound of a gunshot.

Suddenly another student named Clay ran to the front of the class and moved the bodies aside. The SWAT team stormed the room and could be heard shouting: "SHOOTER DOWN!"

In that instant, Goddard realized the gunman had fatally shot himself in the front of the classroom.

The police quickly began triaging everyone in the room. Goddard heard them saying "This person's yellow," meaning wounded, but not critically, and "This person's red," meaning needs immediate attention.

"Then," he recalled, "I heard 'black tag, black tag, black tag.'"

The designation for the dead.

Goddard put his hand over an overturned table to let the EMS personnel know where he was. He was picked up by the arms and dragged out, still fully conscious.

"I never had a direct thought that I was going to die," he said.

His last glance at the classroom was both surreal and unnerving.

There was blood everywhere. Shell casings littered the floor. He saw bodies, although not the body of the shooter.

"The eyes of the police," he recalled, "were so big and wide!"

Goddard was quickly carried out the front door and placed in the grass outside. His jeans and shorts were cut off so his wounds could be assessed. Then, with medical helicopters grounded because of the weather, he was loaded into an ambulance.

The closest hospital, in Blacksburg, was already full of patients. So Goddard and another student who'd been shot were driven 20 minutes down the road to a hospital in Christiansburg, the bouncing of the speeding ambulance causing the pain from Goddard's wounds to intensify.

In the emergency room, doctors were relieved to find that none of Goddard's major organs had been hit. The bullets had shattered into pieces; one had broken his femur. He was given morphine and rushed into surgery.

When he awoke, his worried family and friends were already there. His parents and sister were flown up by a donated private plane from Richmond, where they had just re-located after living all over the world because of their work in international development.

Colin had been born in Kenya, and had lived in Somalia, Bangladesh and Indonesia as a boy. He had been a high school student in Egypt when the Sept. 11 attacks on the U.S. occurred. The irony that he had lived in some of the more dangerous places on Earth, only to almost lose his life on a bucolic college campus in Virginia, was inescapable.

Only in the coming days would Colin Goddard learn the full horror of what had taken place that awful morning of the shootings.

A senior Virginia Tech student named Seung-Hui Cho, a 23-year-old South Korean described as a "tortured loner," had killed 32 people, including the two students, Emily J. Hilscher and Ryan C. Clark, who'd been murdered in their co-ed dorm.

Only seven of the 17 people in Goddard's classroom survived. Kristina Anderson, the girl who had driven to class with Goddard, was one of the fortunate ones. So, too, was Emily Haas, the girl who had muffled the sound of the cell phone with her hair.

Rachael Hill, the girl who'd come to class late, was killed.

So was the teacher, Jocelyn Couture-Nowak. Her body, along with that of another student, was found near the door. Perhaps the two had tried to barricade it—no one knew for certain.

Not surprisingly, Goddard's recovery from his wounds, both physical and mental, would take time.

He was released from the hospital after six days. Yet, instead of heading back to Richmond, he decided to remain in Blacksburg at his off-campus apartment. Later, he would call it one of the best decisions he made in the wake of the trauma he'd been through.

"It was a new house in Richmond—my parents had just moved in," he explained. "I didn't know anyone from there. So I stayed in my apartment with my friends…(and) it seemed like every person I had ever met in college hung out with me, brought me cookies and stuff.

"I was recovering in a community that itself was grieving. Not only would it help me just to be at ease and talk about this and that, my friends would ask what happened, how did you get shot, how were the nurses at the hospital and so on. So I was telling (my story) to them first and not to people I'd never met before.

"Telling my friends helped me get it off my chest . . . Keeping bad stuff inside is a bad deal. (I was) going back to a community that was healing and showing the community itself that there were (shooting victims) that were going to be OK."

Goddard said the second decision he made that helped mightily with his recovery was accepting an internship in Madagascar, which he had lined up before the shooting. The internship was supposed to start in June. This helped him set a goal to physically rehabilitate and be off crutches by then.

"No one knew me there," he recalled of his time in the island nation off the southeast coast of Africa. "I was just some tall white dude with a limp. So I thought this was the biggest thing in the world, to talk about (the shooting) every day and (then go) to a place where it didn't mean shit to the people who lived there.

"They were living with a level of hardship I would never encounter. So getting away from everything helped. It kind of put things back in line."

The third wise decision he made, he said, was to return to campus and get his degree.

He wanted to finish what he had started. But in many ways, this was the most challenging of his post-shooting goals.

"It was incredibly difficult to go back into a classroom," he recalled. "(To) sit in there and hear a kid come in late and slam the door, or someone would burst in past him…my heart would jump.

"Usually there was at least one other survivor in the class with me. And we would look at each other and realize we were freaking out because of that noise."

Goddard said he knew he would eventually be comfortable in class once more, and by the end of the year, he was.

But he said he remains a much jumpier person than he ever was. Loud noises still bother him. He can't watch intensely violent movies. When he's in certain places, he finds himself planning escape routes in case "the shit hits the fan" and another active shooter incident materializes.

In the summer after the shootings, Virginia Tech offered the victimized students a walk-through—along with campus law enforcement—of the classroom where Goddard was shot. The law enforcement officials were there to answer any questions the students might have of what had happened the morning of April 16.

Goddard took the walk-through. He viewed it as another step in the gradual desensitization so necessary to move on from the ordeal.

"They went into as much detail as you wanted," he remembered. "They had diagrams. It helped put the memories in order in my brain. But it was intense. They had stripped the whole room down and filled in the (bullet) holes. I'm glad I did it."

But he declined an offer by the police to let him listen to his 911 call. His parents listened to it instead. And he took a group therapy session with survivors from the French class.

Still, when further therapy for signs of post-traumatic stress disorder was offered, Colin's knee-jerk response was: "'What? I'm good!' Now looking back, I think maybe I should have taken (them) up on it."

Instead, after getting his degree, Goddard plunged into work to strengthen the nation's gun laws, which he called "the next step up on the therapy process" as well as "a way to put that negative experience toward something positive.

"Frankly," he continued, "I admire people who were studying to become engineers and became engineers and didn't let (being victims of the shootings) knock them off their path. But for me, I was a kid about to graduate and didn't know what to do."

For three years, he volunteered for the Brady Campaign to Prevent Gun Violence, the nation's oldest organization formed to reduce gun-related deaths and injuries. In 2010, he was the subject of a documentary, "Living for 32," which told the story of his terror-filled morning at Virginia Tech and how easy it is to buy a gun without a background check in this country.

These days, he's a senior policy advocate for Everytown for Gun Safety, a nonprofit with a mission "to support efforts to educate policy makers, as well as the press and the public, about the consequences of gun violence and promote efforts to keep guns out of the hands of criminals."

Eight years removed from the shootings, he lauds many of the measures Virginia Tech took for the surviving victims, including providing special accommodations for those who'd been about to graduate and getting the survivors together to meet with each other and talk about their ordeals.

But he's critical of the school's failure on April 16 to communicate the heightened danger students faced after the early-morning dorm shootings of Emily Hilscher and Ryan Clark.

"...(The) cops saw a dead student and a dying student and they had a bloody footprint in the hallway, and they started going down the trail of going after the boyfriend," he said, referring to Hilscher's boyfriend, who quickly became a "person of interest" in the investigation. "The school did not alert the community or the student body as to the homicide—almost double homicide—and the unaccounted-for gunman, until just as the shootings in the classrooms broke out."

And while the admissions building and campus communications facility were put on lockdown prior to the classroom shootings, the entire school was not.

"I think if you're not going to put the school on lockdown... you have to let the students know the information (you have) and let them make their own decision," Goddard said. "Had I known there was a dead student and a dying student and an unaccounted-for-gunman before that nine o'clock class—that had happened at 7:40-something—I would not have driven to class that day. It's as simple as that.

"I don't think they did it maliciously," he said of school officials. "It was a mess up. I wish they had fessed up to it. But they never felt they acted inappropriately."

Goddard also took the school to task for treating the shooting survivors who had not been physically injured differently than those who were wounded.

Even though the physically-uninjured had witnessed and experienced many of the same horrors as the wounded, early on they were not paid as much attention to and offered the same opportunities to get together as the wounded survivors. They were also not initially made aware of the opportunities for group therapy and other treatment, leading to a sentiment that services were only for those who had actually been shot.

Lastly, Goddard faults Virginia Tech for failing to admit that perhaps some of its emergency procedures and protocols needed to be re-thought in the wake of the deadly attacks that would forever scar the university.

He recalled that not long after the shootings, the surviving victims and their families met with Virginia Gov. Tim Kaine, school president Charles Steger, and other administration and law enforcement officials.

"One of the mothers," Goddard recalled, "stood up there and said: 'Knowing what you know now, would you have done anything differently?' And the president of the school looked at everybody and said 'No.' And at that point, he lost a lot of the families.

"Certainly, there's a way (for school officials) to protect themselves and not admit liability…No one would have guessed that a double homicide was going to lead to 30 more homicides later. But you *gotta* say, looking back, that we should have done this or that differently now. You *gotta* be able to do that"

Goddard let out a deep sigh and was silent for a moment.

"Maybe," he said finally, "the society we live in prevents people from being able to do that because of the litigiousness of it all."

KEY TAKEAWAYS

1. **Establish an active shooter protocol.** Whether international (Paris) or domestic terrorism (San Bernardino, CA.), lone wolf massacres (Planned Parenthood in Colorado

Springs, CO.) or workplace violence (Fort Hood in Texas), active shooter situations are sudden, deadly, devastating and must be planned for—no exceptions. Again, the first order of leadership is providing a safe place to work and that begins with having an active shooter protocol that is executable during the most intense, violent times that anyone could imagine or experience. There are many sources from which to build a plan, including the U.S. Department of Homeland Security. Research the "Run, Hide, Fight" model.

2.   **Train to standard.** Once a plan is in place, it is imperative the entire organization trains against the plan. You must put everyone through the paces in order to be efficient and create the organizational muscle memory that saves lives. Include your external partners in the planning and training process, including your first responders (police, fire and EMT).

3.   **Lockdowns save lives.** In shootings at Sandy Hook Elementary School in Newtown, Ct. and the Planned Parenthood shootings, it is clear the actions of a few saved the lives of many. There were so many true heroes who selflessly helped others during these critical times. Brisk execution, coupled with composure and patience, will preserve lives until help arrives. Lockdowns must be planned for and relentlessly practiced. Remember, how you practice is how you play. Many studies show that those in public safety and the military react as they were trained in the most stressful of circumstances. You will do the same.

4.   **Be present, connect with all impacted.** As a leader, your presence is imperative when personal safety is on the line. I have clients in the financial services and banking industries. One particular client, an East Coast bank, had one of its branches robbed at gunpoint. No one was injured

but many were shaken-up. Some leaders would not think about going to the branch after that—instead they would empower their subordinates to follow up on the incident. This bank president made it his business to quickly go to the branch and personally interact with and comfort each employee. Years later when I asked some of the employees about the incident, their most vivid recollection was that they had a president who cared enough to be present and empathize. This sent a powerful message, and was the reason that many employees stayed with the bank for so long. The old saying, "People don't know how much you know until they know how much you care" couldn't be more true.

5. **Everyone is a victim.** Just because you have not been shot or injured, doesn't mean you are not a victim. People need to feel physically and emotionally safe. Don't forget about "everyone else" after a tragic incident. Your ability to engage mental health services quickly will not only propel resilience, but is the right thing to do, regardless of cost. People suffer during and after traumatic situations very differently—treat them as you would members of your own family.

6

The Nightmare of a Natural Disaster

Jim and Joanne Hock were never ones to run from weather.

The couple had dealt with many hurricanes and major storms in their 22 years in Bowleys Quarters, a waterfront community in eastern Baltimore County, MD., with a mix of traditional middle-class homes and fancy, modern behemoths that now sell for over $1 million.

So as dusk fell on September 19, 2003, with reports of Hurricane Isabel already churning up the Chesapeake Bay, the Hocks felt they had taken all the precautions necessary to secure their renovated two-story home on Seneca Creek.

"We knew the drill," Joanne Hock recalled. "You batten down the hatches. You put the lawn furniture away. You bring in whatever and do whatever."

But nothing could prepare them for what came next as Isabel, the costliest and deadliest of that year's Atlantic hurricanes, unleashed an 8-foot storm surge that would devastate large swaths of the area's 2,700 homes.

The storm hit Seneca Creek—which opens to the bay—with stunning swiftness and ferocity.

Around 10 that night, the electricity went out, plunging the entire peninsula into an inky blackness. The phone lines were down, too. Meanwhile, the wind was howling, quickly growing in intensity to 75 mph gusts.

By 11, water was coming in the Hock's house and a huge tree on the front lawn fell with a tremendous thud. Earlier, Joanne had tried to call Jim, who was working a night shift for Baltimore Gas and Electric, the local utility known as BGE.

But this was in the era before cell phones were mainstream. At around 2 in the morning, home with sons Nicholas, 16, Zach, 14, and Doug, 11, as well as a neighbor who had fled from a nearby one-story house with her two kids and several pets, Joanne made a command decision: they would all wade out to the Hock's new Ford F-250 and evacuate.

Yet by the time they stepped outside, the water level had risen from their knees to their necks and warning sirens were wailing.

"We'll either be drowned or electrocuted," Joanne thought as they retreated back inside. "We need to stay where we are."

Moments later, she heard her neighbor, Larry Sturla, outside yelling above the wind: "JOANNE HOCK, COME ON OUT!"

Thinking it was a rescue unit in a boat, Joanne yelled back: "We can't come out! There's too many of us!"

But the voice was actually coming from a big Baltimore County diesel truck, with smokestacks on top that allowed it to traverse the rising waters without the engine flooding.

Some 30 of the Hock's neighbors were already in the vehicle. Again, the voice told Joanne to come outside. This time, Joanne told her boys to grab a trash bag, run up to their rooms and return with a change of clothes and whatever item was most valuable to them.

By now, there was two feet of water lapping into the kitchen. The back door had been blown off its hinges and smashed against the wall. In the ensuing chaos, the neighbor's pets somehow got loose in the darkness. Then the Hock's Labrador retriever, Bernie, went out the steps and plunged into the water, disappearing, before being rescued by Nick. The family also brought their pet parrot in a cereal box and hermit crab in Joanne's shirt pocket.

When all the animals had been accounted for, the Hocks and their neighbors held hands and stumbled their way out to the truck with debris whisking by. As the truck rumbled slowly up the road with the headlights cutting through the black night, the evacuees took in a scene of utter devastation.

Water covered the landscape as far as the eye could see. Propane tanks, boats, cars, picnic tables and oil tanks floated everywhere, along with other detritus from the bay's violent purge. All around them were panicked neighbors standing on their roofs waving T-shirts and shouting: "HELP US!"

Joanne Hock recalled: "You're on an open-bed truck! You have nothing with you. And you're driving away from your home, (wondering) if you're ever going to see it again, and what condition it'll be in."

As the truck rounded a curve, Joanne suddenly remembered her elderly neighbor, Maxine Wagner. Wagner was a widow who lived alone and had befriended her sons Nick and Doug.

Two days earlier, anticipating the bad weather, Wagner's daughter had urged her mother to come to her home in southern Maryland. But the stubborn, 80-something-year-old woman had declined, telling her daughter she doubted the storm would amount to much.

"I'll tell her you'll come and get me if anything happens," Wagner had told Joanne Hock.

"Fine," Joanne had replied. "If it does, we'll come get you."

Now, remembering her promise, Joanne shouted for the truck driver to stop.

"If you can envision 75 mph winds, and I am now lying on top of the cab of the truck, screaming into the driver's ear that I need to get off this truck to get this woman," Joanne remembered. "And he refuses to stop the truck.

"I said: 'I made a promise to her. And if you don't let me off, I have three boys on this truck. And if I don't come back, you're raising all three of them!'"

The driver finally stopped.

"Lady, go!" was all he said.

Nick clambered off the truck with Joanne. The water was up to their chins. They climbed over a field of soaking debris to reach Wagner's house. Taking a key off the door frame, they let themselves in and found Wagner sleeping soundly, the water lapping nearly to the top of her bed.

There was no time for niceties. Joanne quickly woke the startled octogenarian.

"Miss Maxine, we gotta get out of here," Joanne blurted. "And we gotta get you dressed."

With that, she whipped off Wagner's nightgown, exposing her teenage son to the unnerving sight of the old woman's saggy breasts.

"Oh, my God!" Nick exclaimed as he dashed from the room. It would be the last comic note of the evening.

After gathering up Wagner's medications and a handful of personal items, Joanne and Nick led her by the arm to the front door. But when they opened it, a wave came crashing through.

The wave hit the old woman in the chest—and she passed out.

"So now we have a full-grown woman, dead weight, and I can't revive her," Joanne recalled. "I've thumped her. I'm a nurse. So we literally floated her and climbed over the debris and got her to the truck, and the neighbor pulled her in.

"She's still out cold. I slapped her and pounded her chest and said: 'Miss Maxine, you need to get yourself together!' Her eyes opened and she said: 'Where am I?' I said: 'You're on a truck and you're leaving your house.' She said: 'I need my checkbook!'"

By now it was nearly 5 a.m. Dawn was beginning to break. The havoc caused by the storm was even more evident. Joanne felt helpless. Her boys were beginning to panic. The truck was passing so many residents crying out for help. Others were fleeing their homes in canoes and kayaks.

As they passed the home of another senior-citizen neighbor, Harriet Chard, Joanne spotted the woman with her face pressed against a window as she plaintively mouthed: "Help me!"

It was a sight that would remain with Joanne for a long, long time.

Soon, they passed several broken down county trucks heading in the opposite direction, back toward the devastation they had just left—and there was Jim Hock, standing in the truck bed of one of them. He had just finished his shift; because of the storm, he'd been slotted out of his typical driver-training duties to haul transformers to Baltimore in a tractor-trailer.

Hearing about the destruction to Bowleys Quarters, he had quickly rushed home to be with Joanne and the kids. Initially, the police had refused to let him back in the neighborhood, saying it was too dangerous.

But, frantic to reunite with his family and fearing the worst, Jim had hitched a ride in on another diesel truck.

"SWEETIE!" Joanne yelled as Jim's truck passed.

But Jim couldn't hear her over the unearthly roar of the wind. So the Hock kids took up the cry.

"SWEETIE!" they yelled in unison.

This time Jim heard them. His face lit up. He jumped off one truck, ran to the other and was hauled up by a dozen willing hands. Years later, he would still grow emotional when recalling how worried he'd been about Joanne and the children on that ride.

Silently he had prayed: "I don't care about the house and nothing else. Just give me her and the kids. God, give me them and I'll be all right. Everything else I can handle. Just don't take them."

Not long after Jim climbed aboard, the truck dropped the shaken evacuees outside the neighborhood. From there, they had a tough two-mile trek to the Safeway, at a nearby shopping center. The Hocks and Maxine climbed into Jim's ancient Crown Victoria and drove to Joanne's brother's house in nearby Overlea.

Only then did the shock of what they'd been through begin to wear off, replaced by the numbing realization of all they had lost.

Their house, which they had finally paid off just two months earlier, was likely destroyed. So was their new Ford truck, as well as the Crown Vic Joanne drove. Their four boats were gone, too.

And so, apparently, was Jim's dream to retire in a couple of years at age 50.

The Baltimore Sun would later report that Isabel destroyed 210 houses in Bowleys Quarters and caused major damage to 632 others. But because of where their house was perched on the edge of Seneca Creek, few families would suffer as much loss as the Hocks.

While Joanne had mostly been a stay-at-home mom for their children, Jim had worked long days at BGE—logging 1700 hours of overtime in one year—to build the house. He had also bought and renovated other homes, and then sold them, to give the family a nice financial cushion.

With a paid-off mortgage, money in the kids' college funds and a new waterfront lot they had just purchased as an additional investment, the Hocks "were in the catbird seat" before the hurricane hit, Joanne said.

"We were ahead of most young people in our age group," she added. "And now it (was) over with. Done. Now it was as if we were new people getting married and starting all over again."

They soon learned that Maryland had been woefully unprepared for an emergency of such magnitude. No help was immediately forthcoming. When the floodwaters finally receded and the Hocks were allowed back into the neighborhood two days after the storm, Joanne burst into tears at the sight of what was left of their home.

To make things worse, her sodden Crown Vic was out front, looking like a ghostly mess. And the couple's new truck was sitting up the road in a big pile of sludge, the cab filled with seaweed and dead fish.

"(Jim) said: 'Cry and then get your act together,'" Joanne recalled. "Which put me back on track."

A close friend, Pat Bosse, drove them back into Bowley's Quarters with his four-wheel drive truck. He had closed his business in Timonium, a small engine repair and rebuild shop, and assembled a gas generator from spare parts which he gave them—invaluable for a family without power.

What followed, though, was an incredible outpouring of support from friends and neighbors. A small army of volunteers, some 75 strong, including policemen and personnel from the nearby fire academy, began helping to shore up the house with lally columns and recover anything that was salvageable, which wasn't much.

The foundation had collapsed. The downstairs level was trashed. All of the oak cabinetry that Jim had so painstakingly restored was ruined. Nevertheless, with the house shored up, the Hocks began planning to live on the second floor until rebuilding was complete.

But that plan was short-lived.

Three days after the hurricane, a representative from FEMA, the federal agency charged with coordinating response to disasters that overwhelm state and local authorities, appeared at the house.

"What are you doing in here?" he asked Joanne.

When she explained her family's plan to live there and rebuild, the FEMA rep shook his head. Then he tapped his watch.

"As of now, you're done," he said brusquely. "I just condemned your house."

He showed Joanne that the home's foundation had shifted dangerously. It was now sitting on six inches of cinderblock, instead of the 12 it had sat on before the storm.

Tapping his watch again, the FEMA rep added: "We'll be back to make sure you've evacuated."

Joanne was left reeling. And once again, the Hocks were left scrambling.

Now they were officially homeless. FEMA was not yet offering any of its emergency trailers; there were none nearby, anyway. Besides, with three boys and a dog, the Hocks would have needed three FEMA trailers.

Jim's parents offered to let the family live with them in their home in Harford County. Joanne's mom said the family could come to the city and live with her. But the boys were going to Baltimore County schools. They had already lost their home; Joanne didn't want to uproot them from their schools, too.

Finally, the partner of one of Joanne's cousins offered them a double-wide mobile home that had belonged to her dad in a nearby trailer park called Sleepy Hollow. With no other choice, they gratefully accepted.

The Hocks moved in thinking they'd be there for two or three months at the most. Instead, they would end up living there for nearly two years.

To say it was not a smooth transition would be a vast understatement. They came in carrying trash bags as their luggage at 11 p.m.

On their first night at Sleepy Hollow, they were startled by a loud pounding on the door at 1 in the morning. It turned out to be one of their new neighbors. Her 30-year-old son had just been in a car accident, and broken both his ankles and wrists. The man had been turned away from a hospital for not having insurance.

The woman pleaded: could the Hocks help get her son into her trailer? They could—Jim and Nick carried him inside.

Two days later there was a letter stuck in the door. This time it was the owner of the trailer park. He had news and it wasn't good: they were being evicted from the trailer park. The park's rules stipulated that only residents who owned their trailers could live there.

Only after the kind intervention of another resident—who put up her mobile home as collateral in the event the Hocks caused any damage—did the owner back down and allow them to stay.

But life at Sleepy Hollow, Joanne would say, "was a nightmare."

For one thing, it was a community primarily composed of seniors. Noise of any kind was frowned upon. This meant the kids couldn't play anywhere in the park. They weren't even allowed to bounce a ball.

Joanne had to put Bernie in the car and take him elsewhere for him to do his business. The Hock's spent as little time there as possible.

The trailer itself was claustrophobic. Depending on the season, either the heat or the air conditioning had to be left on all the time to keep the inside temperature even semi-comfortable.

After the Hocks put up a tree and decorated it for Christmas, they awoke the next day to find their new home covered with praying mantises. The over-heated trailer had caused a nest of the insects to hatch inside the tree.

"They're clear things with black eyeballs looking at you no matter where you were," Joanne recalled. "There were millions of them everywhere. It was nuts."

For the next two years, the Hocks found themselves struggling to navigate the maddening bureaucratic maze that often confronts victims of natural disasters.

They were given FEMA literature and told to visit agency reps set up at a nearby community center and later at the county seat in Towson, but found them to be largely unprepared and unhelpful. On the other hand, the emergency services provided by St. Matthews Lutheran Church on Bowleys Quarters Road proved to be a figurative—and maybe even literal—godsend. The local home improvement association and volunteer fire department were vital to them as well. But, many of the volunteers were also dealing with their own storm-damage issues.

For two solid years, the church provided a daily hot meal and sandwiches for the Hocks and hundreds of other hurricane victims. Volunteers would also bring clothing, toiletries and needed household items to the church for the displaced homeowners, while the Red Cross provided gift cards to purchase shoes and bedding. They also sent a chow wagon in once a day to serve hot dogs and beans.

St. Matthews was equally valuable as a site where the evacuees could network about the best places to apply for aid and loans, and how to fill out insurance forms. It was also a great place for the hurricane victims to commiserate over the incredible bungling of the officials charged with helping them.

The Hocks had both flood and homeowners' insurance, along with vehicle and boat insurance. But applying for payment on both policies, Joanne Hock said, "was the most insane thing we had ever been through. They literally low-balled you."

"The problem with the insurance," Jim Hock added, "was that the homeowners' didn't want to pay for the flood, and the flood didn't want to pay for the wind (damage). And they played against each other so nobody was paid anything."

And when people *were* paid, it often wasn't nearly enough.

Flood insurance is paid by FEMA. According to the Hocks and others, a secretly-recorded video soon surfaced of agency auditors discussing payments to victims, with one auditor clearly heard saying: "Make sure you give them no more than 10 cents on the dollar."

The stone-walling and low-balling were so widespread that the president of the Bowleys Quarters Improvement Association, Mike Vivirito, finally appealed to Maryland's U.S. Senator Barbara Mikulski for help. Only when the outraged lawmaker threatened that FEMA heads would roll did the flood insurance money start trickling in.

When the Hocks finally received enough money to begin rebuilding, they came face-to-face with another scourge of the times: unscrupulous builders bent on making the most of the post-flood chaos.

"They were gouging you beyond belief," Joanne remembered. "Drywall tripled in price. We went through 13 interviews of builders who were charging us $110 a square foot. One of our neighbors, pre-flood, had had his house built for $71 a square foot!"

The Hocks spent the first year after the flood cleaning the debris from their old home, prepping the site for rebuilding, and dealing with still *more* insurance hassles.

When a $24,000 check from the car insurance company went missing for two months, they finally discovered why: with no mailbox at their old address, the insurance people had stuck the check in a plastic bag and hung it on a nail on a post where their mailbox once stood. It was a practice, under normal circumstances, that would result in someone getting fired!

The Hocks spent the second year post-flood building the house, with Jim, who had always been handy, doing much of the work himself. But again, there was a laundry-list of problems.

"Even though we had a builder," Jim explained, "we took everything we could out of contract to make it affordable. Plus the builder wasn't that good. We had to put the staircases in ourselves 'cause he screwed them up three times."

The snafus didn't end there. An electrician with a cocaine problem messed up the electrical outlets. Smoke alarms were never connected. Circuits were put in wrong: when someone used the clothes dryer, the oil burner clicked on.

There were times during the rebuilding when the Hocks wondered if the entire world had gone crazy.

One day, Joanne spent close to eight hours at the county offices in Towson, pin-balling from office to office, seeking signatures for a building permit. When she was finally ushered into the office of the last government drone in charge of such matters, he proceeded to open his desk and fiddle with film canisters from his recent vacation, all the while keeping up an inane patter about being forgetful and not having the film developed.

Finally, she could take it no longer.

"I stood up and said: 'WHAT ARE YOU TALKING ABOUT?!'" she recalled. "I literally grabbed the pen from his hands, put the papers down and said: 'You sign these papers now! I've had enough of your crap! I've been here since 8 in the morning and it's now 4!'

"He handed the papers back to me and I said: 'You're insane! *You* live in a trailer for two years and fight every step of the way.' I said: 'You know what? I hope you never have to suffer through a natural disaster. But you, asshole, I hope your house burns down!'"

Through the long and enervating two years that their family was displaced, Jim and Joanne Hock did whatever they could to lend normalcy to their lives, and the lives of their children.

Just one month after the storm, they returned to their old home site and hosted a block party, complete with a pellet stove in a tent, food (pit beef, ham and burgers) and music for some 100 friends and neighbors.

At Sleepy Hollow, Joanne rose early every morning and drove each of the boys to school in the used Buick the Hock's parents had purchased for them.

And the couple kept their traditional Date Nights going, too. Two of Jim's sisters would always invite Jim and Joanne over, or let them stay in the house when the sisters and their families were away.

"We wanted normalcy for our kids," Joanne explained. "Jim and I knew we were OK. We had each other's backs. When I was worn out and had enough and was frazzled, he was the listening ear. And when he was the maniac, I was the calming person."

Finally, on August 27, 2005, just before the start of another school year, the Hocks moved back into their home on Seneca Creek.

The house was in rough shape, far from being completely renovated. The floors consisted of plywood. There were no shower doors, no molding on the doorways. Makeshift railings were in place simply to get an occupancy permit.

But home had never felt so good.

On the other hand, the financial blow they had had suffered was hard to forget.

The Hocks got an insurance check of only $130,000 from the old house to put on the new house. They took out a mortgage through the Small Business Administration (SBA) and cashed out the boys' college education funds to pay the rest of the building costs.

No longer was going to a pricey out-of-state university an option for Nick, Zach and Doug. (All three would end up attending the Community College of Baltimore County, with Nick and Zach going on to graduate from the University of Maryland, Baltimore County.)

And in his darker moods, Jim would think: "I'll be 78 by the time the mortgage is paid (off.)"

Years removed from their ordeal, the Hocks look back on it with a mixture of awe at the storm's devastation and anger at the needless red tape they were forced to unravel to get their lives back to normal.

Yet there is also a quiet sense of pride in how they came through it.

"It made our kids stronger," Joanne Hock said. "Because they saw we pulled together as a family…For us, the biggest thing through all this was our spirit. You couldn't break our spirit."

Post-script: Jim Hock finally retired from BGE on March 1, 2014 at the age of 58.

KEY TAKEAWAYS

1. **The squeaky wheel gets the grease!** Joanne learned first-hand that the old saw is right: "You learn not to be meek and mild," she said. "You learn: don't take no for an answer." Dealing with many crises, I've always said that people make policies—and people can change them or make exceptions. Find the real decision-maker and artfully, yet relentlessly, state your case until you get satisfaction.

2. **Mobilize, leverage and expand your network.** The Hocks learned very quickly that support and accurate information are critical. In the absence of true direction by anyone in an "alleged" position of authority during this time, the Hocks came to rely on those around them for assistance— neighborhood association representatives, elected officials, church congregants and others who offered helpful tidbits along the way. Whether finding a temporary place to call home or identifying the right person to sign a document, there is no script for how to manage this colossal loss. Build and maintain a strong network to help you obtain information and make sound decisions.

3. **The spirit of giving is alive and well.** For many who are used to helping others from a strong perch, it is often hard to be the recipient of graciousness during a critical time. Allow others to help you—they want to do something and you need the support whether you realize it or not. Typically, those who are used to providing for themselves don't want a hand-out, they want a hand-up.

4. **Insurances, utilities, scammers...oh my!** Practically speaking, always make sure you have the proper insurances to protect your assets—one never knows when disaster will strike. If removed from your home, always put your utility services on hold vs. turning them off or cancelling the service—you will be hit with exorbitant fees if you don't do the former. Watch out for those trying to advantage themselves at your expense. Sadly, there were criminals who made their way to shore by water to loot abandoned homes just after Isabel. Similarly, there were many who jacked up their prices (contractors, service providers, select insurance adjusters, etc.) to exploit families in need. Do your homework and don't fall victim to those who wish to victimize. Don't delegate tasks to others that you can do yourself. Expose and punish those who steal and defraud.

5. **Bond, don't break.** Whether in the aftermath of Isabel, or any number of other hurricanes, tornadoes, earthquakes, landslides, or wild fires, one thing is certain: possessions are lost and families are tested, mightily. In my many years of managing crisis, those who seem to weather the storm over the long haul are families that manage to bond vs. break. Yes, there are times when it is much easier to walk away vs. persevere, but I was struck by the Hock spirit and commitment to one another, and the real impact their adhesiveness had on their children. In fact, one of the Hock boys recently said to Jim, while referring to his own

girlfriend, "I want to have my relationship just like yours and mom's." I cannot think of a higher tribute for Jim and Joanne.

7

Video: The Ultimate Game-Changer

On the morning of Sept. 8, 2014, a grainy black-and-white video appeared online, a video that would shock the world and serve as a swift career-killer for one of the most popular players in the NFL.

Posted by the celebrity gossip and entertainment news website TMZ, it showed Baltimore Ravens running back Ray Rice and his fiancée, Janay Palmer, arguing inside an elevator at the Revel Casino Hotel in Atlantic City, New Jersey.

Seconds later, it showed Rice throwing a left hook that rocked Palmer on the side of her face and sent her crashing to the floor, unconscious.

Life for Ray Rice—and the Ravens players—would never be the same.

"That video changed everything," said Kevin Byrne, the team's senior vice president of public and community relations, when I spoke to him at the team's training facility in Owings Mills, Md. The video also triggered the most visual—and perhaps most embarrassing—crisis in NFL history.

Seven months earlier, another video of Rice had dealt a grievous blow to his reputation as a squeaky-clean role model, anti-bullying spokesman and team good-guy.

That one, posted by TMZ on Feb. 19, had shown the Ravens' star after the spat with Janay emerging from the casino elevator dragging his unconscious fiancé like a sack of grain. Then it showed him stepping matter-of-factly—some would say disdainfully—over her and into the lobby.

According to the Ravens, Rice initially told them that he and Palmer had exchanged angry words in the elevator before she took a couple of swings at him. Then, Rice's story went, he pushed her back, she hit her head on the railing, and fell to the floor.

The Ravens accepted this explanation, wanting to believe in a player as active in the community as any in their history, a gregarious and humble star that owner Steve Bisciotti admitted "we all loved." This was to be expected: as human beings, when we are favorably and emotionally attached to someone, we want to believe the best in that person in most circumstances. So, at the NFL Scouting Combine in February and the league owners' meetings in March, the team spread the word that they believed Rice was a good person who would have his day in court.

They also encouraged him as he pleaded not guilty to assault charges in New Jersey and applied for pre-trial intervention. If approved, this would have helped him avoid prosecution and have the charge expunged if he kept his nose clean for 12 months.

The Ravens wanted Ray Rice back on their team. That was clear from their actions, even when an Atlantic City grand jury delivered a severe charge—felony aggravated assault in the third degree—not just a simple assault charge.

Even with much of their fan base outraged over Rice's original explanation of the argument with Palmer, even with the media skeptical about his version of what took place in the elevator, even with a suspension from the NFL looming over his head, the Ravens were clearing the way for his return.

But it was the emergence of the second video, showing the horrific punch that floored Janay, that would ultimately undo Rice.

Recalling that fateful morning, Kevin Byrne said: "When I come into the office, I'm asked 'Have I seen the second video?' I had not. TMZ has released it. It's now on ESPN. I look at it and (think) 'Oh, my God, that's clearly not the way (Rice) described (the altercation with Palmer.)

"Almost instantly…Dick Cass walks in," Byrne continued, referring to the Ravens' president, "and he says 'We have an issue.' I said 'We do.'"

The issue demanded immediate attention and there was little doubt as to how it would be resolved.

Ray Rice's days as a Raven were as good as over.

"He can't be on our team," Byrne said, summing up management's thinking after seeing the second video. "No. 1, it's not what he said happened. And, two, someone who's done this can't be on our team."

After a quick meeting of their crisis management team—Bisciotti, Cass, general manager and executive vice president Ozzie Newsome, and Byrne—the Ravens issued a statement saying they had released Rice.

His five-year, $35 million contract, with three years left on the deal, was effectively terminated.

Less than an hour later, the NFL suspended Ray Rice indefinitely.

As of this writing, he remains a pro football outcast.

The Ray Rice saga remains one of the starkest examples of the power of video to galvanize attention to an issue, shape public opinion and alter forever—or even destroy—careers.

It's safe to say that video has changed the world. Today, most people would rather point, click and watch a video on their computer or mobile device than read an article online, in a magazine or in a newspaper.

Virtually everyone has the ability to record video through their mobile devices, leading to an all-time rise in the phenomenon known as "citizen journalism." As we've seen, though, this can have a dark side. How many times have we heard of a citizen failing to respond to someone in need, choosing instead to continue recording that person's plight or demise in the hope of getting credit for shooting the video of the day? How many "likes" one can get is seemingly more important than helping another during a life-changing moment. It is sickening.

Video has changed professions and industries, from instant replay and officiating challenges in sports to the way police departments increasingly require that their officers wear video cameras to record their dealings with the public.

Before the prevalence of video, people read about domestic violence issues or police-involved shootings. Now they see and hear these events regularly via shared video and audio files. As in the Ray Rice case, despicable violence is brought to life quickly and it tends to immediately shape public opinion more viscerally.

As we know now, it can make humiliating and cringe-worthy events linger in the mind's eye for months.

Imagine if there had been video of the incident that reportedly triggered the Tiger Woods sex scandal: his wife, Elin Nordegren, swinging a golf club and chasing the groggy golf star in the wee hours of the morning after learning of his infidelities.

Conversely, it seems that when the public can't "see" the alleged offense, it's forgotten more quickly, due to the inability to bring the incident to life again and again.

Ironically, it was another highly-publicized "elevator video," this one involving the hip-hop megastar and music entrepreneur Jay Z, that offered the Ravens a measure of hope in the early days of the Ray Rice scandal.

Three months after Rice's incident, surveillance video taken inside an elevator at a New York hotel captured Jay Z being assaulted after a party by Solange, the sister of the rapper's wife, Beyoncé.

But the video showed that despite being kicked and swung at wildly, Jay Z did nothing more than fend off Solange by grabbing her foot. There was no evidence that he ever attempted to strike her.

So when the Jay Z video was first leaked by TMZ, "in my mind, I'm thinking a little about that" in relation to Rice's case, Byrne said.

Without having seen video of what took place between Rice and Palmer *inside* the elevator, all the Ravens could do was hope their player had acted in as restrained a fashion as the famous rapper.

Instead, the world would learn via the second Revel video that he had not.

Now, that video will live in perpetuity. It will follow Ray Rice everywhere, even when he makes positive news.

As Rice and his people know, he has an albatross around his neck, one that he'll have to work incredibly hard to shed. And only time and distance from the incident will allow that to happen. The platform of pro football, to amplify his message, would accelerate that goal.

In the short-term, however, he has suffered mightily from the blurry images that captured his left fist flashing and the horrific assault on Janay Palmer.

From all reports, his marriage to Janay (they were wed in a private ceremony the day after his indictment was handed down) endures, with both partners determined to make it work.

But his career lies in ruins.

Although he says he's had overtures from several organizations, not one of the other 31 teams in the NFL has made a serious effort to sign him.

When asked if he thought this was a direct result of the ruinous effects of the video, Kevin Byrne nodded emphatically.

"Clearly. It's the video," he said. "If you sign Ray Rice, he'll become the lead story across the world again. 'Cause it's easy video for all the networks. It's news. You sign him, it's the video (being shown again.) He scores his first touchdown, it's the video. He becomes a dominant player again, it's the video. His team goes to the playoffs, it's the video.

"So if you're a (team) owner sitting there and weighing the decision to sign him," Byrne continued, "you're thinking: 'Can't we get someone *close* to Ray Rice?'"

As I've preached as long as I've been in this business: video doesn't allow us to forget—ever.

KEY TAKEAWAYS

1. **Don't rush to judgment.** I have been in countless crisis team meetings where at least one person tries to either dismiss or diminish the severity of the issue, while remaining hopeful that no one will ever find out. Or the feeling is that all of the relevant facts have been gathered, even if the event happened only 24 hours earlier. When the Baltimore Ravens saw the first video of Rice dragging Janay out of the elevator, seemingly unconscious, everyone knew there was another video inside the elevator which would show what actually happened—the events which led to her being rendered unconscious. In an industry now built around instant replay and video production at all angles, neither the Baltimore Ravens nor the NFL waited to impose a two-game suspension before they knew the whole story. Identify whatever reason you want for this oversight: rush to judgment, money, team performance, the 'Ray's a good guy' drumbeat, and so on. The bottom line is that imposing sanctions before having all of the facts is such an incredibly dangerous and slippery slope, because you are "going all in" when the stakes are at their highest. In other words, you are placing all of your reputational equity at risk based on someone's word when you really don't *know* the all of the facts.

2. **People hedge the truth or lie while under scrutiny. Believe it!** Knowingly or unwittingly, many people have a strange way of "misremembering" the exact truth while under duress. Do not cave into the pressure of automatically believing someone's initial recounting of the facts because you will get burned. Process is as important as outcome, so relentlessly pursue the truth. In this digital age, seemingly more times

than not, an audio recording, photographic image or video file provides more perspective, even in the most intimate of settings—ask Donald Sterling, the disgraced former owner of the NBA's Los Angeles Clippers. Take advantage of technology to either prove or disprove an allegation.

3. **Sound character is not negotiable.** The Baltimore Ravens, while seemingly duped by Rice's account after the release of the first video, fired him without hesitation the second time around. Many say it was an easy decision; yes, but also an emotional release. Use critical times such as these to learn from the past and set the character bar even higher; your organization will benefit over the long term. There is no substitute for good character—it's not negotiable.

4. **Rebuild quickly, even when a dark period is required.** Rice is not getting any younger and his window for getting a chance to restore his career closes even more quickly each day. Rice must be public, he must continue to show remorse and talk about how he has turned this incredibly horrible incident in his life into a lesson he can use to help others. The former leader of anti-bullying efforts in Baltimore went from being loudly applauded at every public appearance to having fans sell his jersey for a free cheesesteak at some of Baltimore's street corner eateries. Crisis recovery is brand building and Q ratings (a measure of familiarity and likeability) are important.

5. **Put your money where your mouth is.** If he wants to get back in the public's good graces, Ray Rice must invest in domestic violence and conflict resolution programs. He must channel energy into helping others learn from his mistakes and be very transparent in doing so. America is a forgiving society if people, on the whole, truly believe one is remorseful and deserves another chance. The question is whether a franchise owner is willing to take the risk and thrust his team

into the Rice spotlight, even if the former running back has a fresh set of legs and a legacy to rebuild. Domestic violence is a very serious issue around the world. While overcoming and rebuilding is never easy, Rice, so far, seems to have focused on the right things first—himself and his family. As for his profession, he must employ the same sense of vigor and intensity off the field as he did on. Even if Rice never plays professionally again, he has a platform to help others if he truly wants to make a difference in this world.

6.   **Take Responsibility and Rebuild Quickly.** For the past two decades, the Ravens' organization has been extremely inclusive and invested in the greater Baltimore community. After recognizing the initial shortsightedness of their actions, Bisciotti and team officials acted quickly to re-route their message and restore trust, to women in particular. Bisciotti publicly said he was embarrassed that his team placed domestic violence on the same level as other infractions.

"I think that we were pretty stupid not to recognize domestic violence as a category by itself," he said in a 2015 ESPN interview. Through a letter to season ticket holders, Bisciotti acknowledged the team's shortcomings - he did what great leaders do and took responsibility. The team continues to commit educational and financial resources to support domestic violence initiatives, along with many other community-based efforts. The silver lining in all of this is the very important issue of domestic violence was put on the front burner and new league policies have been created to address it. As a very visible and influential sports property that initially fumbled on the Rice issue from a crisis leadership standpoint, the league can be an even stronger anti-violence advocate for women with the appropriate leadership will.

KEY CONCEPT

Reputational Elasticity

In 2012, Starbucks found itself taking a major PR hit in the United Kingdom.

The gourmet coffee shop chain faced a huge public outcry, including a well-orchestrated boycott for not paying enough taxes despite making enormous profits. According to media reports, using a clever—and perfectly legal—dodge, Starbucks had paid only £8.6 million in taxes since opening its first store in the UK 14 years earlier. The figure seemed ridiculously low, especially when it was revealed the chain had amassed £3 billion in sales over that time.

Boycotts and protests took place at over 40 locations. The chain was hammered unmercifully on social media. Facing a fierce level of competition in the industry, Starbucks saw its sales drop. Soon enough, it offered to pay even more in taxes than required. And as the months went by, it desperately spent inordinate amounts of time and money repairing its sullied reputation.

The lesson in all this?

Reputation matters.

It's estimated that over 60 percent of market value is based on reputation alone, according to the public relations firm Weber Shandwick. Reputation is one of the most important, yet often underestimated, aspects of doing business today. When a crisis occurs, time and money are spent very quickly, not only dealing with the situation at hand, but defending and then repairing the reputation as well.

The fact is, consumers have access to more information about the products they buy and the companies they support than ever before. A simple product search reveals much more than company-controlled data on a website, and certainly more than the information provided on product packaging. Recent reviews, newspaper articles and historical information about the product on the Internet all influence the reputation of its company.

Which brings us to the term "reputational elasticity."

Elasticity of Demand is an elementary economic concept that describes a consumer's willingness to buy a good or service when the price of the good or service increases. Reputational elasticity is a product of demand, and it is in direct proportion to how many choices an organization's stakeholders (read: consumers) have.

Many choices mean higher elasticity, while fewer choices equal lower elasticity. With higher elasticity, a consumer is less likely to purchase the product or service as the price increases. Demand is described as inelastic when a consumer will buy the product at almost any price.

Reputational elasticity of demand is very similar, with an organization's reputation replacing price as a determining factor. A company that sells products or provides services that are easily available elsewhere has high reputational elasticity, making it much more vulnerable to a hit on its reputation.

And since coffee-drinking customers can go just about anywhere to get their caffeine fix—from Caribou Coffee, Costa Coffee, McCafé or Dunkin Donuts to the swill that brews 24/7 at convenience stores—Starbucks was particularly vulnerable to a damaged reputation.

Interestingly enough, Google and Amazon were also accused around the same time of not paying their fair share of taxes. Their tax dodge involved a complicated scheme that ran products and profits through Ireland and Luxembourg, according to brandindex.com, which measures brand perception among the public.

But the brand-tracking service said Google and Amazon's reputations suffered less of a hit.

"As online companies, Amazon and Google experience less reputational elasticity due to indirect consumer relationships," brandindex.com reported. Reactions and protests are harder for consumers to coordinate, measure and participate in.

"Both companies also provide services that have fewer competitors. Amazon's customers are less willing to stop using a Kindle or search for equal choice while Christmas shopping. Google services have an incredibly low number of competitors and consumers do not pay directly for many of its products. Even as an email provider, the difficulty of switching providers renders Google consumers almost completely inelastic."

A positive reputation is an asset and something organizations must seek to build relentlessly over time, even though it may be hard to quantify its value or risk in dollar amounts.

Research shows that a sound reputation is important to investors and share price. It is equally or more important to consumers who will choose to buy a product or service based on their perception of a company. When stakeholders are surprised or disappointed by an organization, they share the news and respond.

Weber Shandwick reports that the top five elements consumers discuss among themselves are:

1. How they feel about a product they've purchased (69%).
2. The quality of a company's customer service (55%).
3. How specific companies treat their employees (45%).
4. News about a scandal or wrongdoing at a company (55%).
5. How one feels about a company as a whole (40%).

Consumers learn about companies through discussions with others and make purchasing decisions based on reputation, Weber

Shandwick says. In fact, 88 percent report that word of mouth is the most important factor in their opinion of an organization, while online reviews (83%) and online search results (81%) are the next most important factors in shaping opinion.

Reputation matters because consumers now have a vast amount of control over it, and that influence is becoming more recognizable by executives. In the Weber Shandwick study, executives estimate that 60 percent of their firms' market value is attributable to its reputation and nearly 86 percent of executives have increased their efforts to build reputational capital in recent years (www.webershandwick.com/news/article/the-ceo-reputation-premium-a-new-era-of-engagement).

As the legendary investment guru Warren Buffet says: "It takes 20 years to build a reputation and five minutes to ruin it. If you think about that, you'll do things differently."

Smart CEOs think about it all the time—they are the ultimate gatekeepers of their brand.

Sure, an organization's reputational capital is based in part on what the organization says and does, but more so on the things its stakeholders think and say about it. Reputational capital is accumulated over time like a savings account of goodwill that reflects the values of an organization and its image in the marketplace.

During a crisis, reputational capital is a bank of trust from which an organization will draw, particularly since the 24-hour news cycle and Internet spread information incredibly quickly. Anyone with an internet connection and recording device can wreak havoc on your brand.

Foodprocessing.com, which bills itself as "The Information Source for Food and Beverage Manufacturers," estimates that news of an emerging crisis spreads within an hour 28 percent of the time, and the bad news spreads within 24 hours 68 percent of the time.

So how do you measure an organization's reputational elasticity? For the purposes of reputation protection and defense during a crisis, several factors are most important in determining an organization's or corporation's risk:

Highly-Competitive Industry. Competition is key in assessing reputational elasticity. Since consumers are self-educated and involved in the products they buy and the brands they affiliate with, a variety of choices in a marketplace mean that during a reputational crisis, they won't hesitate to align with another brand, or to vote against a company by spending their dollars elsewhere. Retail, food and fuel companies, financial institutions, transportation, tourism and healthcare concerns are just a few of the thousands of industries in this category.

Crisis-Prone Industry. In 2014, the Institute for Crisis Management counted more than 223,000 crisis news stories in almost 10,000 news outlets. More than 414,000 people lost their jobs, including over 50 executives, in no small part due to the continued expansion of social media's influence on spreading negative news, as well as poor crisis handling. For example, among the industries most affected by data breaches were major retailers and educational institutions. A record-setting amount of money was paid to whistle-blowers in 2014, particularly in the financial and healthcare industries, according to the report. The transportation industry accounts for the most casualties, both in aviation and railway accidents around the world.

During a major crisis, the outcome and costs, including time, money and careers, are largely driven by how the crisis is managed, since the suddenness with which the crisis occurs makes planning difficult. Mismanagement further contributes to the deterioration of an organization's reputation.

Direct Relationship with Consumers. Since consumers are such an important part of the creation and perpetuation of reputation, companies that have a direct relationship with the end user of their product or service tend to experience higher elasticity. A trucking company is an example of an industry where the end user of a product may be unaware of how a product reaches store shelves. Trucking companies are generally business-to-business, meaning that their reputation elasticity will be lower than that of a company that deals directly with individual consumers. This doesn't mean that business-to-business organizations have reputation inelasticity, but that the other factors are more important in determining their threat level in a crisis.

Reputational Capital. Regardless of an organization's ranking in the above categories, there are companies that have very high or very low reputational capital. Low reputational capital means an organization has nothing to draw on during a crisis and stakeholders are likely to switch to a competing product or service soon after a crisis breaks. Conversely, organizations with high reputational capital already have a positive relationship with stakeholders, and can expect their stakeholders to take the time to learn about the crisis before taking their dollars elsewhere. A bank of reputational capital helps lower elasticity, giving organizations a chance to respond well in a crisis and protect its assets.

Remember, customers quickly share news and vote with their feet. In today's marketplace, it is not uncommon to see a "boycott" page affiliated with a company or brand. The ability for consumers to mobilize for or against you, both digitally and traditionally, happens more quickly now than ever before. Stakeholders will leave you for another brand experience in a hurry, particularly when encouraged by the wisdom of another consumer (testimonial). Understand how elastic your brand is—what the customer options are and how easily can they jump ship. Most importantly, why would a customer leave to support a competitor? What are the key trigger points? You must know this about your product or service. Understanding your brand elasticity will drive strategy, shape future decision-making and help you navigate risk.

8

Create Organizational Muscle Memory

On the cold afternoon of January 15, 2009, Capt. Chesley "Sully" Sullenberger nosed US Airways Flight 1549 into the clear skies above New York's LaGuardia Airport.

Less than four minutes later, after a "bird strike" from a flock of Canadian geese knocked out two of the jet's engines, he coolly and skillfully made an emergency landing in the frigid Hudson River that saved the lives of all 150 passengers and five crew members, earning him international acclaim and admiration.

"Within eight seconds of the bird strike," Sullenberger wrote in his book "Highest Duty," "realizing that we were without engines, I knew this was the worst aviation challenge I'd ever faced. It was the most sickening, pit-of-your-stomach, falling-through-the-floor feeling I had ever experienced."

As to how he was able to focus and execute his duties during one of the most compelling dramas in modern airline history, the answer—personal heroism aside—was surprisingly simple.

"My life is all about routine. It's about checklists and procedures," he said in a training video not long after his ordeal. "Be prepared for the unexpected by doing the little things day in and day out. You ready yourself for the big things…"

Clearly, what Capt. Sullenberger relied on heavily during his ordeal is a concept that I teach and call organizational muscle memory. This applies to corporations and businesses as much as it does to everyday citizens in all walks of life.

In the context of preparing for, navigating through or recovering from issues of sensitivity, adversity or crisis, there's no question that—to use the old cliché—people play how they practice. And what Capt. Sullenberger and his co-pilot did in those nerve-wracking moments in the sky high above New York was begin working their way down the checklist of airline emergency response procedures put in place for just such an event.

They were doing what they'd been trained to do, and they followed the protocol as it was laid out to them and drilled into their heads for decades.

Immediately after Flight 1549's engines failed, Capt. Sullenberger took over the controls of the crippled aircraft from First Officer Jeff Skiles, who began handling the emergency checklist.

Sullenberger quickly focused on the three general rules of any aircraft emergency:

Maintain aircraft control, analyze the situation and take proper action, land as soon as conditions permit.

As detailed in his book, there is also a variation on those rules that pilots find easy to remember: "Aviate, navigate, communicate."

"Aviate: fly the plane," he wrote. "Navigate: make sure your flight path is appropriate and that you're not flying off course. Communicate: Let those on the ground help you, and let those on the plane know what might be necessary to save their lives."

Also aiding him was this: as a young pilot in the Air Force, he had studied aircraft accidents to learn from the experiences of the pilots involved.

"Why did pilots wait too long before ejecting from planes that were about to crash?" he wrote in "Highest Duty." "Why did they spend extra seconds trying to fix the unfixable?"

Sullenberger's many flights from LaGuardia in the past had also given him an encyclopedic knowledge of the terrain he was flying over, as well as the distances to the nearest airports should he attempt an emergency landing at one.

In the end, his training, military experience and geographical knowledge would help him conclude that all four nearby airports (LaGuardia, JFK, Teterboro and Newark) were unreachable by the damaged aircraft.

Not to be discounted in any re-telling of what happened to Flight 1549 that day is that Capt. Sullenberger had the perfect demeanor to handle the stress of the moment.

When you think about leadership, you think about composure. This was a case study in pilot composure if ever there was one.

As the aircraft flight lurched and dropped through the skies, Sullenberger would write in his book, the badly shaken passengers in the quiet cabin reacted in a variety of ways. Some prayed. Some texted loved ones.

A U.S. Army captain and his fiancé kissed and told each other "I love you" and "accepted death together." A management consultant from Charlotte, North Carolina thought about how he was his mother's only surviving son, and that his death would no doubt kill his mom, too.

A man who had survived a near-deadly incident on a plane some 20 years earlier took out a business card and wrote "I love you" to his parents and his sister and thought: "This could be the end of my life. In 10 or 20 seconds, I could be on the other side, whatever the other side will be."

But Capt. Sullenberger remained calm and focused on the task at hand, which was to avert a catastrophe either above or in one of the busiest cities in the world.

In any crisis, people look for direction. Absent that direction, presented in a composed manner, chaos will ensue.

But there was no sense of that on Flight 1549.

As he continued to struggle with the damaged plane, Sullenberger radioed air traffic control and said, in a remarkably even voice: "We may end up in the Hudson."

In fact, the aircraft was already descending below the tops of Manhattan's skyscrapers toward the wide, sparkling river.

Too busy in the early moments of the emergency to fill in the passengers on what was happening, he now intoned: "This is the captain. Brace for impact!"

Attempting to control the aircraft without critical engine thrust, he nevertheless guided it to a hard, slightly nose-up landing. After that, he supervised the emergency evacuation of shivering passengers out onto the wings of the sinking plane, where they were quickly helped into a flotilla of rescue boats.

Perhaps as much as any pilot in history, "Sully" Sullenberger had proven to be prepared for the ultimate crisis of his career.

"One way of looking at this might be that for 42 years, I've been making small regular deposits in this bank of experience, education and training," he concluded during a "60 Minutes" interview with Katie Couric after his Flight 1549 heroics. "And on Jan. 15, the balance was sufficient so that I could make a very large withdrawal."

In many ways, businesses should do the very same thing to prepare for a crisis.

All organizations should strive to be systems-driven versus hero-driven to cope with adversity.

In other words, there should be policies, protocols and training mandates in place to respond to any crisis that develops. These policies, protocols and training mandates should be reviewed periodically, because how you practice for a crisis is how you plan—and how you "play"—when faced with a calamity, when it really counts.

Heroes emerge, generally, due to the systems and training each organization has in place. If organizations rely solely on the hope that a hero will emerge—and Chesley "Sully" Sullenberger was most definitely a hero—they'll be lucky if one actually does.

But most times in a crisis, there is chaos and no leadership. Which is why companies must continuously go over their "checklists" and relentlessly train and prepare to meet the moment—just as the military does, just as law enforcement does, and just as fire and paramedics do.

Even if it's a moment they hope will never come.

KEY TAKEAWAYS

1. **Perform a crisis audit.** Businesses must create a systemic, not heroic, approach to dealing with issues of sensitivity, adversity or crisis. Immediately engage in a crisis audit, a comprehensive evaluation of what will cost you time, money, customers, careers and, in the worst of scenarios, lives. Take a look from within your organization and across the industry, as the best predictor of the future is the past. Once a prioritized issue list has been created, work your way down the list to reduce your points of exposure. There is no doubt in my mind that playing defense for offensive-minded companies is a way to preserve long-term success. The most important elements of any organization's longevity, particularly when confronted with issues that disrupt business continuity, are to establish effective predictability, planning, training and execution mechanisms. The crisis audit will identify various points of organizational exposure and assist in reducing corporate vulnerability.

2. **Create a checklist.** A crisis checklist is paramount because companies can't create—and people don't read—operational policies during crisis. Develop checklists so people can manage during times of crisis, particularly when they're being overwhelmed emotionally with bad news and are struggling simply to respond. During a critical time of

need, people must act with precision and confidence. In order to drive confidence, most employees want to know they are acting within policy, even during emergency circumstances. An accessible, executable checklist allows for quick, confident activation.

3. **Be direct.** There is often a tendency to soften words or not be direct with ominous news. My experience is that, while the news might initially be shocking, people prefer the bottom line right away. Ironically, I call the bad habit of not being direct "circling the messaging runway" vs. landing the plane. Do not circle the runway with negative or emergent news, immediately land the plane and tell people what is going on. You will earn their confidence and trust more quickly. Also, when you *do* deliver the tough news, be certain you have some direction for your audience, as they will need to understand all that I've outlined in the Resilient Moment Communications Model.

9

Apologize?
Is it Heartfelt or a Hoax?

Congressman Anthony Weiner stonewalled for days before finally expressing remorse and admitting he'd sent lewd photos to a number of women he'd met online.

Golfer Tiger Woods waited almost three months to address the burgeoning sex scandal engulfing him, then offered a cryptic explanation before a hand-picked audience, with the few media members in attendance forbidden to ask questions.

"NBC Nightly News" anchor Brian Williams delivered a quick "I'm sorry" at the end of an evening broadcast, admitting his story about being on a helicopter that was fired upon in Iraq was untrue and claiming he had "conflated" it with a ride taken on a different chopper.

And Chip Wilson, founder of yoga-inspired clothing company Lululemon, took to YouTube after complaints about his company's apparel and expressed regret—not to his customers, but to his employees, who now had to deal with the whole mess.

File all four of these under: Possibly the Worst Apologies of All Time.

My feeling is that a heartfelt, timely and thoughtful *mea culpa*, with a high degree of connectivity to those who were adversely impacted, is extremely important for anyone who has screwed up.

But all too often, handlers of high profile figures try to script and rehearse the apology until it no longer seems genuine. It comes across as theatrical as opposed to meaningful, with a less than high degree of authenticity.

In other words, a hoax!

And that's where people get in trouble.

This was certainly the case with Tiger Woods, whose public apology in 2010 in the TPC Sawgrass clubhouse in Ponte Vedra Beach, Fla., struck many as stilted and emotionless. He read his 14-minute statement as if he were giving a high-school speech.

Not once, in my opinion, did you feel the level of humility and sorrow you'd expect from a person who had put his wife and family through an embarrassing tabloid scandal linking the 34-year-old PGA great with a seemingly endless list of strippers, porn stars and party girls.

I can tell you this: people don't often remember what you say in an apology, but they do remember how you made them feel. And the immediate reaction to Woods' remarks was a shrug from most of us and a collective *meh.*

Obviously, he was still being evasive about the events that took place.

What was the real story of the car crash he'd been involved in the previous November, when his wife Elin Nordegren had reportedly discovered his serial cheating and chased him from their Florida mansion while swinging a golf club?

Tiger didn't say. Nor did he talk in any detail about the lurid behavior that had led to his stunning downfall and the disastrous aftermath that had seen big-name sponsor after big-name sponsor cut him loose.

All in all, the feeling was that he had run the tightly-managed news conference with all the transparency of a Third World despot.

"He might as well have done this on YouTube," former sportscaster Pat O'Brien said on CNN's "Larry King Live." "But I do think that he's got to subject himself to some sort of question-and-answer at some point."

Bottom line: Tiger's remarks—even the stunning revelation that he'd spent 45 days receiving in-patient therapy for sex addiction—did nothing to rebuild his image.

One thing I've noticed over the years is that most people don't apologize until they feel there is no other option. They're always assessing the legal, business or political risks first, instead of focusing on apologizing because it's the right thing to do based on their own moral compass—and the need for the aggrieved parties to hear a mea culpa.

Case in point: Anthony Weiner, the seven-term Democratic congressman from New York.

When a lascivious photo of his bulging underwear—purportedly sent by him—first surfaced on the Internet in the spring of 2011, he claimed someone had hacked his Twitter account.

In the ensuing uproar, which included days of mocking national media coverage and outraged reactions from his constituents and Democratic party leaders, Weiner kept dodging questions about his conduct.

He said he couldn't say with "certitude" that the photo was of him. He alluded to someone playing a prank on him. He was non-committal as to why he hadn't gone to the police to report his hacked social media account.

Undoubtedly, he was weighing how much the fallout from his actions would jeopardize his congressional seat. It was a classic example of a politician having just two sides of the brain: get elected, get reelected. Not all, but many politicians I've met over time seemed more concerned about decision-making optics vs. acting in the long-term interest of those who entrust them to serve.

Even though the pressure to explain Weiner's actions was

unrelenting, it was a week before the married lawmaker finally apologized for lying about the photo. In flat, emotionless tones, he also admitted that he'd engaged in "inappropriate conversations" and "exchanged messages and photos of an explicit nature" with women he'd met online.

There's no question that most of us associate a visible show of emotion, or even the slightest of lip quivers, with a genuine apology.

In 2009, when two Domino's Pizza employees in North Carolina posted an online video of themselves smearing mucus on sandwiches, putting cheese up their noses and performing other disgusting acts with food, the company faced a huge PR crisis.

Initially, Domino's executives were slow to react and shrugged the issue off to being a local franchisee concern. And, in the category of "no bad story ever gets better," one of the employees in the video was a registered sex offender. But when company president Patrick Doyle took to YouTube and delivered an impassioned apology, the crisis abated and sales rebounded.

"It sickens me that the actions of two individuals," Doyle said, staring intently at the camera and fairly spitting out the words, "could impact our system where 125,000 men and women work for 812 local owners around the U.S. and more than 60 countries around the world.

"…We're taking (this) incredibly seriously," he continued. "Nothing is more sacred to us than our customers' trust."

As for Anthony Weiner, when another lurid photo of him was released by a radio talk show host, Weiner resigned from Congress two weeks later.

But that was hardly the end of his sexting troubles.

In 2013, while running for mayor of New York and hoping to rehabilitate his image, he delivered another bombshell announcement at yet another news conference. This time he confessed that he had continued to send explicit messages and lascivious photos of his now not-so-private parts to young women on the Internet.

Perhaps even more embarrassing, he admitted to doing this using the pseudonym "Carlos Danger." As you could imagine, the New York tabloids had a field day with the moniker.

Facing the media this time, with his nervous and embarrassed-looking wife, Huma Abedin, at his side, Weiner hurriedly read his apology as if it were a check-in-the-box, something he *had* to do as opposed to something he really meant.

I don't think an apology should *ever* be read. It's OK to rehearse your remarks. But, looking your audience in the eye and speaking from the heart will always make for the most authentic apology. Americans are very forgiving, as long as they know the person looking for forgiveness is truly contrite.

Brian Williams' apology, delivered in the waning minutes of his nightly newscast in February of 2015, was an unmitigated catastrophe. I consider it one of the worst I've ever seen.

For one thing, the high-powered anchor deflected all blame for what seemed to many an obvious attempt to exaggerate his role in the incident.

Insisting he "conflated" or misremembered the events that took place in a helicopter over the Iraqi desert in 2003 was a way of saying "I made a mistake" versus saying "I did something wrong."

I lied to make myself seem more heroic. Those were the words that outraged Iraq War combat veterans—and much of the rest of us—wanted to hear from Williams.

Instead, his cavalier-sounding apology earned him even more widespread criticism and ridicule. So did his effort to characterize his remarks as a "bungled attempt by me to thank one special veteran," the pilot of the chopper he'd flown in, "and, by extension, our brave military veterans."

Within days, he was suspended without pay for six months. When an in-house investigation revealed at least a dozen more embellishments, he was eventually stripped of his anchor role on the prestigious "NBC Nightly News." Four months later, it was announced that Williams would return as a breaking news anchor on MSNBC, a significant demotion for someone once considered the network's shining star and perhaps the most visible newsman in the nation.

There's an old saying: it's not the crime, it's the cover-up. Brian Williams learned this lesson first-hand. The problem was, he seemed to be a serial offender.

The country watched him dip a tentative toe into the pool of apology and say: will that cover it? And when it didn't, when there was blow-back, he waded in a little deeper until he found himself in way over his head.

In terms of damage done to both his persona and his brand, Williams' apology was right up there with the notorious Internet mea culpa delivered by Lululemon CEO Chip Wilson in November of 2013.

Initially, during an interview on Bloomberg TV, Wilson said the so-called "sheerness" of the company's yoga pants was probably caused by women who were simply buying pants that were too small for them.

Are you kidding me?

Then, doubling down on this theme, Wilson added: "Frankly, some women's bodies just don't actually work" for the pants. "It's about the rubbing through the thighs."

It was one of the more cringe-worthy statements any clothing company head has ever uttered, all but communicating to a segment of Lululemon customers: "Hey, fatsos, maybe you shouldn't buy our workout gear!" This was the height of insensitivity.

Faced with the predictable uproar over his remarks, Wilson then posted a bizarre video on YouTube in which, seemingly on the verge of tears, he apologized to…well, not to any of the female customers he might have offended.

"I'm sad for the people at Lululemon, who I care so much about, that have really had to face the brunt of my actions," he intoned. "I take responsibility for all that has occurred and the impact it has had on you. I'm sorry to have put you all through this."

"How Not to Apologize, With Chip Wilson of Lululemon" read the headline of a blog item in *The Washington Post* a few days later.

I couldn't have said it better myself.

KEY TAKEAWAYS

1. **Reputation translates to real dollars and professional longevity.** In this global world of transparency, the reputation of a chief executive or "face" of an organization has never been more important. One of the more interesting studies I found during my research was a previously released study by Weber Shandwick (in partnership with KRC Research) entitled *The CEO Reputation Premium: Gaining Advantage in the Engagement Era.* The study surveyed more than 1,700 executives to better understand what is required of leaders today. One key finding: 44% of marketplace valuation is based on the reputation of the CEO. And, according to the study, strong marketplace valuation helps organizations attract investors, generate positive media attention, sustain crisis, and attract and retain employees. Based on my client observations, this is not only true, but tested during crisis and any resulting apologies. Put another way, whether a pope, president, police chief or politician, do you trust their words and actions, particularly when an apology is delivered? If not, while their personal and professional equity plummets, so does earnings per share. Please, if you are going to apologize, be sincere and don't underestimate your stakeholders' ability to move your marketplace value needle.

2. **Never read an apology!** You wouldn't read an apology to a person in a face-to-face setting, so why in the world would you do it in any other environment? During Ray Rice's apology on live television, he read from notes on

his iPhone, which routinely timed-out. He ping-ponged his attention between the iPhone screen and reporters—enough to jumble even the smoothest communicator's train of thought.

3. **If you don't mean it, don't apologize.** Too many people in this world apologize because they feel cornered and feel they have no other option. They apologize to appease the aggrieved parties, or to simply salvage or advance their own, selfish agendas. We hear this reaction all the time: "They're only sorry because they got caught!" Please, if you really don't mean it, don't do it…but if you do, remember that you are never too big to apologize. There is something really refreshing and likable about someone who puts his or her hand in the air, accepts responsibility and humbly does the right thing. It's the right thing to do!

4. **Apologies decrease litigation.** The medical industry has learned this concept; others should research, with interest.

KEY CONCEPT

To Err is Human,
To Forgive Divine

Apologizing: lessons from one industry

There are an estimated 98,000 deaths due to medical errors each year, the equivalent of ten jumbo jets crashing each week. Likely that figure could be closer to half a million deaths yearly, according to the Journal of Patient Safety, because many medical mistakes go unreported or underreported.

One such story involves the newborn twins of actor Dennis Quaid and his wife, Kimberly. Dennis called Cedars-Sinai Medical Center to check on his premature twins one November evening in 2007 prior to going to bed. The newborns, Thomas and Zoe, were being treated for infections a few days after they had come home from the hospital. Their doctor had recommended taking the babies to Cedars-Sinai for treatment. Dennis was assured by the nurse that evening that everything was fine.

Nothing could have been further from the truth.

According to the Los Angeles Times, two hours before the phone call, a nurse had noticed Zoe oozing blood from an intravenous site on her arm and another on her foot. That is when the doctors knew something was very wrong.

It turns out, as part of the treatment for their infections, both newborns were given heparin, a blood thinner. Instead of the recommended dose, the babies were given 1,000 times the recommended amount, a mistake possibly made because the bottles of the different doses were very similar in size. The overdose had left the twins› blood too thin to clot, leaving both babies vulnerable to uncontrollable bleeding.

As hospital officials rushed to save the babies' lives, no one notified the Quaids of the crisis. In fact, Dennis learned of the episode at 6:30 a.m. the next morning when he was greeted in the babies' hospital room by someone from the hospital's risk management team, a doctor and nurse. As Dennis said in an interview, "Our kids could have been dying, and we wouldn't have been able to come down to the hospital to say goodbye."

From a crisis perspective, the number of mistakes from the situation is astonishing. Medical decisions had been made without the Quaids' knowledge. Someone had leaked the medical mistake to media outlets, so the paparazzi were everywhere, even trying to deliver gifts. Also, hospital administrators were always in the babies' room. Kimberly said: "They wouldn't let us be alone with our children, to the point where we were just like, 'Can you please just give us a moment?'"

Another report by state regulators found Cedars-Sinai had placed the Quaid twins and others in urgent jeopardy by improperly handling medication. Cedars admitted to "at least three separate safety lapses," according to reporting by the *Los Angeles Times*. At least one other child had also received an overdose of the same drug.

The twins spent 11 days in intensive care. While the twins have fully recovered, the Quaids said in interviews they felt "betrayed and misled" by Cedars-Sinai. Dennis turned the experience into an opportunity to advocate for patient safety and started The Quaid Foundation, testifying before Congress on the need for greater tools to prevent medical errors.

Although the twins survived, they are two of the hundreds of thousands of patients harmed by preventable medical mistakes. In fact, "health care harm," if hospital-acquired infections are included in the count, is the third-leading cause of death in the United States. "The amazing part about it is, it's preventable," said Quaid.

The one thing the Quaids did not hear in the first few hours after the error was: "I'm sorry."

There is a movement called "Sorry Works" to get more medical professionals to say those words after a mistake. In order to avoid or reduce the risk of doctors getting sued for malpractice, there is an effort to go to a softer, kinder model, including apologizing when a medical error has occurred. Offering an apology, especially when coupled with an upfront settlement offer, has had a significant impact in reducing legal costs for some hospitals.

A study conducted in 1994 reported that 37% of patients and the families who had filed medical malpractice suits said "an explanation and apology were more important than monetary compensation, and that they might not have filed suits had they been given an explanation and apology." In one example, the University of Michigan Health System has been encouraging doctors to apologize for mistakes, and found that when they did, annual attorney fees dropped from $3 million to $1 million. Malpractice lawsuits and notices of intent to sue also fell from 262 filed in 2001 to about 130 per year after initiating the apology practice.

Dr. Michael Woods, a surgeon in Colorado and author of "Healing Words: The Power of Apology in Medicine," said he learned from his own experience the impact of actions and inactions. Woods was overseeing surgery to remove an appendix when a resident punctured an artery, leading to a more complex operation. The patient reported that how Woods handled the aftermath had a significant impact on her emotions. In one instance, he propped his feet up on the desk and acted as if he did not care, according to the patient's recount. Woods claims he wanted to apologize, but legal advisers recommended against contact with the patient when the patient threatened a lawsuit.

According to the National Council of State Legislatures, as of 2014, over 35 states had enacted "I'm Sorry" laws that prevent acknowledgements of remorse, expressions of sympathy, condolences or apologies from being used against medical professionals in a court of law. This allows medical professionals to make these statements in earnest without worry that the admission could later be construed as an admission of guilt. The legislation is directly related to help reduce medical liability/malpractice litigation, while also a nod to the fact sometimes people just want to hear, "I'm sorry."

10

"Gerry with a G.
No relation."

It started as a simple case of mistaken identity. But for Gerry Sandusky, the long-time sports director at WBAL-TV in Baltimore and radio play-by-play voice of the NFL's Baltimore Ravens, none of what followed was ever simple.

Instead, his life would devolve into a months-long cycle of hate mail, death threats on social media, strangers cursing him in public and his anxious family struggling to cope with an ordeal they could never have imagined—all because his surname was the same as the most notorious pedophile in recent memory.

For Gerry Sandusky, the nightmare officially began on November 4, 2011, a date forever seared in his memory.

Arriving at BWI-Thurgood Marshall Airport for the Ravens' charter flight to Pittsburgh—Baltimore would play the arch-rival Pittsburgh Steelers the next day on "Sunday Night Football"—Sandusky checked in as usual at the team's security area.

"Hey," the guy behind the counter asked, "did someone in your family get arrested?"

"Not that I'm aware of," Sandusky replied.

After all, he had just talked to his brother Jim that morning. There had been no mention of anyone in trouble with the law.

"The Penn State football coach?" the counter guy persisted.

Oh, Sandusky thought, momentarily relieved. Over the years, he had often been asked if he was related to Jerry Sandusky, the veteran assistant to the legendary Joe Paterno on the Nittany Lions coaching staff.

"No," Gerry told the counter guy. "No relation."

Maybe, Gerry thought, the other Sandusky had been popped for a traffic violation or some other minor incident that made the news.

But on the Ravens' charter, Gerry could feel the eyes of half the people on the plane trained on him.

Finally, his producer called up the story of the other Sandusky on his cell phone.

"Uh-oh," the producer said, "you have a problem."

A *huge* problem, as it would turn out.

Just hours earlier, Penn State's Jerry Sandusky had been arrested on 40 counts of sex crimes against young boys. The indictment by Pennsylvania Attorney General Linda Kelly, handed down 24 hours earlier, had come as a result of a three-year investigation.

Not until later that evening, after an uncomfortable dinner in a Pittsburgh hotel where he sensed people avoiding him, did Gerry Sandusky get details about the sensational case unfolding in western Pennsylvania.

Turning on the TV in his room, he watched a half-hour program that spelled out the lurid allegations against the Penn State assistant and ticked off the charges: seven counts of involuntary deviant sexual intercourse, eight counts of corruption of minors, eight counts of endangering the welfare of a child, seven counts of indecent assault and a slew of other offenses.

As the full magnitude of the case became clear, Gerry Sandusky was horrified.

"I thought: oh, my God!" he recalled. "By the end of it, I'm nauseous. To hear your name, or what sounds like your name, (associated) with this heinous crime…"

Thank God, he thought, that his mother had named her youngest son Gerry with a G, even though every other brother had a name that started with J.

Nevertheless, he knew much of the general public, especially outside Baltimore, would barely notice the different first-name spelling of his name as media accounts of Jerry Sandusky's abominable crimes riveted the country.

"It was a little like being in the first 10 minutes of the movie and knowing exactly how the next two hours were going to go," Gerry said.

Predictably, things got no better the next day.

On the field an hour before game time, Ravens coach John Harbaugh informed him that many of the Ravens players were wondering if it was Gerry—or his father or his uncle—whose arrest now dominated the news.

And a few minutes later, when Gerry stuck out his hand after being introduced to Dick Ebersol, the president of NBC Sports, Ebersol flinched noticeably and pulled his hand back after hearing the name Sandusky. The network exec quickly excused himself and disappeared from the sidelines.

"It was *so* uncomfortable," Gerry Sandusky recalled. "People literally didn't want to be seen with me. Especially people being photographed. I (knew) what was going through their heads. All of a sudden, (for me), it was: pariah.

"I was rattled," he went on. "The thing that made it so difficult, having worked in television for so long, I knew it wasn't going away in a couple of days. I knew this would be years. I knew it would be a burden on my family. I knew this was a tsunami-caliber crisis."

When he arrived back home the next day, Gerry sat down with his family. His wife, Lee Ann, was still reeling from the sickening stories out of Penn State and bracing for the backlash sure to hit her family. Their daughter Katy, a sophomore in college, and his son Zack, a 10th grader in high school, were also worried.

But Gerry, drawing on his life's experiences, had already formulated a plan to cope.

"Here's how we're going to handle this," he told them. "We're not going to react. People are going to say all kinds of horrendous things. We're going to be proactive on social media, we're going to be extremely cordial, we're going to keep our cool."

It was a lesson he had drawn from his father, John Sandusky, a long-time football player and coach. The elder Sandusky had been an assistant coach on the 1969 Baltimore Colts team that, despite being heavily favored, lost Super Bowl III by a score of 16-7 to the New York Jets and their brash star quarterback, Joe Namath.

In school the next day, young Gerry had gotten in a fistfight with a boy who'd taunted him about the Colts' loss.

Hearing about this, John Sandusky had sat his son down and delivered a pointed message: There are a lot of jerks in this world; you can't punch them all without becoming the biggest jerk.

But John Sandusky's family would later be tested by a tragedy far greater than a mere loss in the Super Bowl. When Gerry was 17, his 19-year-old brother Joe, a linebacker for Tulsa University's football team, died of sepsis.

"It blew-up my family," Gerry recalled. "Seven years later, my mother died of cancer, which is really just the manifestation of heartbreak."

What he was facing now, Gerry knew, was nothing compared to Joe's death.

"I told my family: that stuff prepared me for this," Gerry said.

Now, with his wife and kids around him, he settled on the response they would give to anyone who confused him with the notorious child molester.

It was simple and to the point: He was "Gerry with a G. No relation" to the monster at Penn State. End of story.

"You let me put this on my shoulders," he told his wife and kids.

"I don't want you taking the heat for this. Don't worry about me. I'm going to protect you."

Along with his father's wisdom, he drew on the teachings of Gandhi, Martin Luther King, Jr., and Jesus, as well as the philosophy of non-violent resistance. He also recalled what he'd learned from Stephen Covey, author of the best-selling self-help tome: "The 7 Habits of Highly Effective People."

"He said that between action and response, there is a space," Gerry Sandusky recalled. "And while you can't control the action, if you use that space, you can always choose your response. And the more you choose your response, the bigger that space gets."

No, there would be no flying off the handle when the haters mistook him for the other Sandusky and cursed and jeered him.

And, oh, did the haters come out.

At the height of the abuse, he was getting 400-700 tweets a day, plus emails and letters, inviting him to die and rot in hell for all eternity.

A month after the scandal broke, Gerry and Zack were doing Christmas shopping at a mall when a man, accompanied by his wife and two sons, spat vile comments at Sandusky as he passed.

Another man, this one elderly, snarled: "I didn't think they let rapists out to do Christmas shopping."

If ever there was a moment to shelve Gandhi's pacifist teachings and go full-blown thermonuclear on someone, this was it.

But Gerry Sandusky resisted the impulse.

"There's clearly a part of you—your lower self—that wants to reach down their throat," he said. "But all I did is just stare at them. Without a word, I let them digest what they had said to me in front of my son…I watched them crumble."

Both men sought him out a short while later to apologize after discovering they'd lashed out at the wrong Sandusky.

Then, there was the time Katy was in a bar in Towson with her college friends when a guy sitting nearby saw Gerry on TV delivering his sportscast and began loudly insulting him.

"You need to stop that," Katy warned the blowhard. And when he didn't, she hauled off and punched him.

"I understand," Gerry said later after his daughter had told him what she'd done. "But that's not how we're dealing with this."

Still, the strain of being linked—however peripherally—to an appalling series of sex crimes would take its toll on the entire family.

One Saturday night, Gerry and Lee Ann were lying in bed, watching TV, when a "Saturday Night Live" sketch about Jerry Sandusky came on. Gerry found it funny. His wife did not. Instead, she rolled over a few seconds later, folded herself into the arms of her husband, and started crying.

"That was when I realized the depth of how much it had hurt my family," Gerry said. "Intellectually, you know this is going to be tough for them. But emotionally, when you feel their pain at that level, that's where it took everything I had to maintain our course: 'We're going to be a lighthouse, not a courthouse.'

"...I never wavered from that approach. Because I...knew this was going to be the greatest teaching lesson of my life, to show my children that there is a way out of the darkest moment, in which you don't have to compromise who you think you are."

But some well-meaning people *did* want him to compromise, in effect.

"Just change your name," they would tell him.

Sure, that was the easy thing to do, at least in the short term. But Gerry Sandusky says he never considered the option. It was his family name. He and his wife and kids were proud of it.

And what if he changed his name and then *that* name became linked to another heinous crime? After all, he told *The Baltimore Sun:* "Somewhere there is a plumber named Bernie Madoff. Somewhere there is a salesman named Ken Lay (Enron). And somewhere there is a truck driver named Charles Manson. And they'd have to live with this."

As it happened, Gerry Sandusky and his family would live in the shadow of the other Sandusky's crimes for months.

With each new development in the case—the initial arrest, the investigation, the firing of the venerated Paterno, the controversy surrounding the removal of his statue from the campus, Jerry Sandusky's sensational trial—a new wave of abuse would hit Gerry's Twitter feed and email account.

Not until the convicted sexual predator was finally sent off to prison did things begin to quiet down.

Even to this day, though, Gerry Sandusky gets comments on his surname, especially when he's out of town doing Ravens broadcasts or speaking engagements.

Perhaps the lone positive to emerge from the ordeal, he says, is that once he's introduced to someone, that person never forgets his name.

But the negatives far outweigh any benefit that came his way. There is the psychological scarring his family has endured, for one thing. And he's also certain he's been passed over for jobs since the Jerry Sandusky scandal first made headlines.

When his contract at WBAL-TV in Baltimore was up, Gerry said, he began exploring other job opportunities, among them, taking his broadcasting skills to the next level. At least one TV executive was quoted as saying Gerry was definitely good enough to do network play-by-play, but that he would never be hired with a last name of Sandusky.

Nevertheless, as difficult as it was, what Gerry Sandusky tried to do from the very beginning was to keep what he was going through in perspective.

"What I tried to share with my family was: we're not victims," he said. "There (were) real victims in this story. We (were) inconvenienced. There's a big difference. So don't be a whiner, be a winner. The world doesn't need more whiners."

KEY TAKEAWAYS

1. **Plan your work, work your plan—stay the course.** Once a plan to deal with the negative backlash was put in place, Gerry and his family remained true to their vision, conviction and the plan's execution. This was key. Staying the course is huge in any crisis, once a plan is defined, and as long as it's effective. Mid-course correction is necessary at times. But the plan Gerry had was very straightforward, easy to understand and execute. In fact, it had tremendous shelf life.

2. **Tap your experience, trust your gut.** Gerry drew on two important experiences in his life to get him through his ordeal: his father's Super Bowl loss and the untimely death of his brother. People must draw on their own personal experiences, or the experiences of others, and trust their gut when going through crisis. Many times, your first thought is the best thought. Trust yourself.

3. **Create and use your "space" wisely.** We know we can't control what others do, but we can control our responses and reactions. And, if you use that "space" Gerry refers to wisely, you can always choose your response. Let's face it, immediate, emotionally-charged reactions more times than not foster regret. From permanently damaged relationships to terrible acts of violence, getting caught up in the moment changes lives, and not often for the better. Remember, people will often not remember what you said, but they will remember how you made them feel.

4. **Focus demands sacrifice.** There is a marketing concept I've always remembered: focus demands sacrifice. That is, focus on the message, image or memory you want people to remember and cut the rest, whether it's the Nike swoosh or "Gerry with a G. No relation." It is imperative

to communicate quickly, succinctly, passionately and in a way that is easily consumed, understood and repeatable. Your message point ripple will travel further.

5.   **Humor provides connectivity and a quick out.** Gerry's situation was no laughing matter. There are times, however, when using small doses of well-timed humor can be appropriate, and can help one cycle through an awkward moment before anger takes over. So, if your name happened to be Martha Stewart while you lived in New York City in the early to mid-2000's, you may have heard a few sneers and chuckles when you introduced yourself. At that time, Martha Stewart, the home-decorating mogul, was indicted for securities fraud. In fact, she was tried and ultimately found guilty of several charges, and ended up in prison. Someone also named Martha Stewart back then might have deflected a jeer of "Are you going to cook for all those inmates?" with a quip of "I think they'd really like my fall menu, especially the bread and water dumplings." If you get angry at every dimwit who tries to have fun at your expense, you will exhaust yourself and plunge into a rage-filled hole that quickly deepens with each comment.

11

The Impact of Spiritual Leadership

Joe Hart remembers the moon that night. It was full and luminous as he drove to the hospice in the pre-dawn hours, wondering what he would say to a cancer-ravaged woman who had slipped into a coma and was now near death.

Hart is the chaplain and director of spiritual support services at Greater Baltimore Medical Center (GBMC), a busy 245-bed facility in the suburb of Towson, Maryland where some 28,000 surgical procedures and 53,000 emergency-room visits are recorded annually. (I have a strong affinity for GBMC as my mom nursed there for 40 years before her celebrated retirement—postpartum and labor and delivery was her life's calling.)

The woman Hart had gone to see—a 59-year-old whom we will call Joanie—was a lapsed Catholic who had struggled to find spiritual solace in the midst of her illness. Hart had earned her trust over the years after many difficult conversations about faith and God, during which she remained a reluctant skeptic.

"I'm yearning to believe, because I'm trying to find an anchor to hold onto," she would tell him.

Hart would nod sympathetically.

"I know that God...has touched my life again and again," he would answer. "I found that in my journey and those crossroad experiences of my life, I had something to hold on to. My prayer for you is that at some point God will reveal this to you."

Arriving at the hospice room that night, Hart found Joanie's family gathered around her. He sat next to her bed and held her hand. She was still comatose, but warm and breathing steadily.

"Joanie, it's Joe," he said in a low, soothing voice. "I want you to remember our conversations over these years. I believe God will reveal God's self to you."

Hart considers himself a Death Coach, or End of Life Coach, "in the best possible way," he hastens to add. He had been with many dozens of people who had died while in a coma. He was ready to be of service to another.

Now, with moonlight streaming through the window—"the brightness was just amazing," he would recall—Joanie began to take her last breaths.

"And all of a sudden," he recalled, "she just smiled! I mean, she *smiled!* And she wasn't strong enough to squeeze my hand. My belief is that Jesus will reveal himself to you. She died shortly after that. She was very much at peace.

"It was," he continued, growing emotional at the memory, "one of the hallmark moments of my career. You had to *feel* it to believe it."

Talk to people like Joe Hart, who has worked at GBMC for 22 years and been in ministry for 32 years (he's an Episcopal priest), and they'll tell you that spiritual leadership has never been more important than it is today.

"The continuum for me is that crisis happens in every generation, the comings and goings of life," he said. "The difference today is how families face them and handle them."

Forty years ago, the landscape of the typical American family looked far different than it does today.

"Generationally, there was always a built-in system of support, no matter what happened in life," Hart says. "My grandfather on my mother's side had 13 brothers and sisters. My grandmother had nine brothers and sisters. My father's side had extended family, with many living within blocks."

"So when crisis came back then, there was built-in support. 'I'll make sure the kids get home from school, you start their homework,' when family members had babies or went into the hospital. For generations, families had that gift."

Sadly, far fewer have it today.

Families aren't as stable as they once were, Hart says. They're smaller and more separated. According to Hart, the Gallup Organizations tells us the average American child now lives 150 miles from his or her home of origin. The average American family has 2.5 children.

All in all, the typical American lives longer than ever, but with far fewer people to depend on should a health crisis occur. Despite the amazing advances in technology over the past 10 years, study after study shows that vast swaths of society are more isolated and lonely than ever before.

"And while we have all these hand-held devices," Hart said, referring to smartphones and iPads and the like, "people are not in contact as they used to be."

Yet a major health crisis, such as the ones hospital staffers see every day, can overwhelm even the closest of families.

It can also change the family dynamic in an instant, making the need for spiritual leadership even more important.

When I interviewed Hart for this chapter, he was helping comfort an 84-year-old man whose world had just turned upside down.

While standing in the mail room of his condominium, the man had suffered a freak injury when the ball joint of his hip had suddenly, and painfully, dislodged. Over the years, the man had built a thriving family business, which he'd passed down to his son, and he'd been a devoted husband and member of his Lutheran church.

But now, he was a patient at GBMC, having nightmares as a result of his recent hip surgery and the residual anesthesia in his system.

Anxious, tearful, he asked Hart to sit and pray with him. He said he wanted to "refocus" that God was near.

Hart asked the man about his fears, his struggles, his questions about life going forward. It soon emerged that what was weighing on the man most of all was his sense of responsibility, cultivated over a lifetime, and his new sense of powerlessness.

"I'm the head of this family, I built this business and here I am, the most vulnerable one in my family," he told Hart. "Here's my poor wife, she's had to come every day bringing me clothes. I just want to get out of here. But I can hardly stand up."

The bottom line: he could no longer take care of himself. As a life-long provider for those around him, he was now vulnerable and afraid.

This is the type of fearful lament healthcare professionals hear every day. It's also one that spiritual advisors like Hart are uniquely trained to deal with.

"To me, the spiritual leadership piece is how to negotiate these transitional moments of life as families are confronted with them on a daily basis," he told me. "One thing of our human condition that we...just take for granted is the pattern of our lives, that we're going to get up, we're going to get to work, we're going to earn our pay, we're going to do what we're called to do.

"And then a crisis comes in the middle of this like an explosion. And now it's: 'What the heck am I going to *do*?' To me, that's where spiritual leadership becomes crucial. Because I believe we become the bridge between that which is known and that which is unknown. We become the bridge between that which is assured and that which is in question.

"Chaplains become the bridge," he continued, "between that which is solidified in a family history, a family way of being, and a new way of interacting."

Spiritual leadership of this sort—intensive, nurturing, selfless, done year after year after year—is not for the faint of heart.

Joe Hart routinely works 50 or 60 hours a week providing care and guidance to patients who are often staggered by some of life's most horrific moments.

He was called to the ministry, he says, because of the influence of his family, which he depicts as deeply religious and kind-hearted.

In his neighborhood, friends and neighbors brought food and drink to families dealing with sickness or death. He grew up at the tail end of a time when the dead were often laid out, prior to burial, in their homes, with friends and family members invited to pay respects and keep vigil with the family.

As a boy, with instructions from his mother, young Joe would often slip quietly into the kitchen of a grieving family and leave a casserole dish on the stove, with a note expressing deepest sympathy from the Hart family.

Those formative years laid the foundation for the endless reservoir of empathy that any spiritual leader worth his salt must have. And the best of them develop an almost instinctual way of guiding people through crisis by cutting to the crux of a problem and arriving at a possible solution.

When a dying, elderly man was rushed to GBMC and ended up in the intensive care unit, his family sought Hart's advice on whether to allow the man's 7-year-old grandson, a boy named Billy, to see him.

Billy adored his grandfather. The two were very close. But the boy's mother was afraid the sight of the failing grandfather—gray-skinned, unconscious, hooked to several machines, with tubes running in and out of him—would be too traumatic for the boy to handle.

Yet earlier, the family had also mentioned to Hart that the grand-father seemed to be "hanging on," almost waiting for something to happen before he died.

"Maybe he's waiting for Billy," Hart mused.

With the family's permission, Hart got a candy bar and took a walk with Billy. The boy was chatty and cheerful.

They talked for a few moments, about baseball and the Orioles and the old man's train collection. His granddad, Billy told Hart, was his best friend in the whole world.

"Billy, your granddad's very sick," Hart said to the boy. "But you know he loves you very much. If you were given an opportunity to tell him one more time that you love him, would you want to do that?"

"You bet!" the boy replied.

Patiently, Hart explained to the boy that his granddad would likely not look the same as he remembered. Now he'd be in a big hospital bed, with nurses hovering around him and tubes supporting him in different ways.

But Billy was still keen on seeing the old man, and Hart thought he would handle the visit with the support of his parents and other family around him.

"He's a 7-year-old boy," Hart advised Billy's still-anxious mother. "He's not going to see tubes. He's going to see his *grandfather*."

Ultimately, the decision was made to let Billy in the room. And as soon as he walked in, he went over and touched the patient and exclaimed: "Granddad, it's Billy! Can you see me? I love you, Granddad!"

Billy's Granddad was still unconscious. But his heart monitor registered a brief, but noticeable, uptick at the sound of the boy's voice.

After a minute or two, Billy was ushered from the room. And not long after, his grandfather died peacefully.

For Hart, it was another wondrous moment in a career filled with such moments, when simple and effective spiritual leadership truly makes a difference in someone's life, and death.

"That's why I love what I do," he said, getting teary-eyed once more.

Even when their efforts are initially rebuffed, the best spiritual leaders persevere and attempt to form some sort of human connection with people in the throes of crisis.

Years ago, when he was a young chaplain, Hart appeared in the hospital room of an elderly Jewish woman who was dying of cancer.

"Chaplain, before you say a word, I'm not a believer!" the woman cried.

"A believer in what?" Hart asked.

"A believer in God," the woman said.

"OK," Hart replied, "what else do you believe in? You seem like an interesting person. Tell me more about your life."

The woman was still cautious, but the two began to talk. In the course of the conversation, she told Hart that she had worked for years in the traffic division of Baltimore's Department of Transportation.

"Are you telling me that if I'd known you back then, you could have fixed some of my parking tickets?" Hart asked jokingly.

"No, I don't think so," the woman replied, still with a serious demeanor.

But her guard was down now. She was beginning to warm to this friendly, open chaplain. And when the conversation turned to the things the terminally-ill woman valued in her life, she became emphatic.

"You know what I love?" she told Hart. "Renaissance art."

After that, Hart recalled: "We started talking about her favorite artists. And now we got into the spiritual realm."

An artist himself, Hart had a book at home called "Artists on Art." It consisted of the journal entries of artists over the span of seven centuries in which they discussed their art, its origin, meaning and purpose.

"What would you think if the next time I visit, we read some passages from the journals of some of your favorite artists?" Hart asked.

"Oh, I'd love that!" the woman answered.

And so it was that a creative, hard-working chaplain found a way to bring solace—and spiritual nourishment—to a terminally-ill patient who had wanted no part of his presence just days earlier.

One of the last journal entries Hart read to the woman was by the French impressionist and modernist Henri Matisse.

The subject, fittingly enough, was tranquility:

What I dream of is an art of balance, of purity, of serenity, devoid of troubling or depressing subject matter. An art which might be for every mental worker, be he a businessman or a writer…like a mental soother, like something good, like an armchair in which to rest from physical fatigue.

"She drew comfort from that," Hart says, "and she died a few days later. For her going back to the art world, her spirituality was really about beauty. But (the challenge) was about finding that spirituality. I believe everybody has it…"

Toward the end of my long conversation with Joe Hart, I asked him why people reach for spirituality during dark times—at any stage of their lives. He paused for a moment before answering.

During a crisis, he said at last, "many people realize there's something out there beyond themselves. When one is vulnerable, they very much realize that they can't solve this by themselves. So I think it's just the human realization of that.

"And they think: 'Where can I go to be supported? Where can I go to find solace? Where can I go so I'm not alone in the midst of crisis?' To me, the common thread is a hunger for something beyond ourselves."

As for those in his line of work, Hart says the number one gift spiritual leaders can give to those in crisis is what an old mentor called "the essence of presence."

"My Irish mother," he added, "always said: 'Never underestimate your presence at a funeral. Or, in the presence of someone's life.' What she was getting at was this: It's those simple gestures of love that have an impact over time.

"Ninety percent of ministry is presence. It's just showing up. And to me, that's a core spiritual leadership principle."

KEY TAKEAWAYS

1. **Connect empathetically with those struggling.** A major

challenge today is teaching the next generation to be compassionate and loving—in person—as the personal touch is disappearing quickly due to technology. People issue apologies via text, communicate their emotions through technology, and have lost the art of looking one another in the eye and communicating with authenticity, particularly when they're on the wrong side of an issue. I firmly believe that empathy is the best attribute a leader can have. While research supports this observation, I can tell you that from working with countless leaders, those who can empathize under any circumstance are often the most effective at driving desired outcomes. In my view, the most effective leaders are driven by a sense of mission and love for others. We are all human and very much share the same emotions.

2. **Have faith in a higher being or larger purpose.** When a person is on the brink of—or embroiled in—crisis, keenly focusing on taking care of one's mind, body and spirit is critically important. Spirit, in particular, becomes even more essential when people feel they've lost control of a situation, particularly their health. I can't tell you the number of times I've worked with a troubled leader where that person's renewed sense of spirituality, or belief in a larger purpose, helped him or her navigate a personal storm. Many report having emerged stronger than they were before crisis hit. In fact, many believe in giving one's troubles to their God or relinquishing to a larger purpose. My mom often used to say: "Rob, things will happen exactly as they're supposed to." Sometimes, you just have to have faith in an outcome that you ultimately don't control.

3. **Depend on others for perspective—you can't do it alone.** Hart described spiritual leadership as the bridge between the known and unknown. Many people have great difficulty dealing with the unknown, and in my business,

everyone involved in a crisis is searching for known resolutions—quickly. They are used to being in control and spend inordinate amounts of time, money and other resources searching for quick answers. The inability to find these known resolutions leaves them with a feeling their life lacks control and predictability. Turn to others for perspective and insight during life's most difficult times. Candidly, crisis is a time to ask for help from others. I have had to get by the "ego barrier" of so many people to make them understand that embracing humility and turning to someone else for perspective is a core strength, not a weakness. Turn to others, you never quite know where the answers to your problems lie.

4. **The only thing constant in life is change—accept it.** The benefit of growing older and having more life experience is truly understanding that nothing on this earth is forever. Life's crises will certainly impact us during our journey with one another. Whether with impending death, physical health, mental health, financial challenges, divorce, addiction, job loss, incarceration, home loss, loneliness, accidents, bullying or even a general sense of diminishing self-worth (the list goes on and on), we all deal with life's challenges. However, the most resilient people I know are able to optimistically find a path forward after sincere personal acceptance. They are able to take personal inventory, accept their situation, focus on controlling what they can and find satisfaction in smaller, incremental steps toward stability. Perseverance is key, but accept life, *your* life, first.

5. **Power of prayer.** Throughout my life's journey, I have heard and read about the power of prayer—believe in it. During life's most difficult times, mobilize the prayer warriors as miracles do happen.

12

Do You Have The Moxie To Be A Crisis Leader?

Early one morning in 2002, when I was working at the Governor's Office of Crime Control and Prevention in Towson, Maryland, I stopped by to see the boss.

After knocking lightly on his office door, I let myself in.

But this time, Stephen P. Amos wasn't sitting at his desk as usual.

Instead, I found him sprawled on the floor with his eyes closed, suffering from an excruciating migraine attack.

Given what Stephen was going through at the time, the fact he was enduring skull-splitting headaches was hardly shocking.

That year, soon after taking over at GOCCP, a little-known state agency that provided access to federal and state grant funds to improve public safety, Stephen's world had turned upside down.

Out of nowhere, he found himself at the center of a high-profile public corruption probe, wrongly accused of improperly using grant money for administrative purposes. As a former law enforcement officer and U.S. Justice Department official, Amos had never been under investigation, for any reason. And, knowing what I knew about Amos, I knew he would find it *repugnant* to subscribe to any wrongdoing.

Since the GOCCP was overseen by Lt. Gov. Kathleen Kennedy

Townsend, a Democrat in the midst of a heated race for governor against Republican Robert L. Ehrlich, many suspected a political motive behind the charges.

Townsend, in fact, called the probe, led by Republican U.S. Attorney Thomas DiBiagio, "political garbage."

Nevertheless, it would drag on for another three years until federal prosecutors suddenly dropped their indictment of Amos in 2005, citing an obscure legal opinion they claimed would have made it difficult to win a conviction.

Thus, ended one of the most painful ordeals I have ever seen a colleague go through—a man I knew to be of the highest moral character, a man who had been unfairly targeted and was innocent of even the slightest wrongdoing.

But in the months that the investigation dogged him, I also watched Amos continue to perform superbly at his job, put the well-being of his worried and dispirited staff above his own and deliver one of the most inspiring examples of crisis leadership I've ever seen.

"A lot of tears, a lot of pain," Stephen said of that difficult time when we met not long ago for drinks and dinner.

Before the crisis hit, he continued, "a lot of my decision-making had been about what was in my best interest (and for) my career path. But I soon came to realize it was no longer about me.

"I realized I had a much bigger responsibility. I had to start thinking about the larger team, how to bring them together, how to communicate that there was a future, that the sky's not going to fall and you're not going to crumble."

The first hint of trouble for Amos came in early 2002, as Maryland's gubernatorial campaign entered its final crucial stages. He began to hear rumors of a possible federal investigation into the GOCCP.

One day around that time, I received an odd phone call from Stephen.

"Rob, we're friends, right?" he asked with a slight chuckle.

"Of course we are," I said.

"Well," he went on, "do you have any idea why the FBI is in my office?"

At first, he professed not to be overly concerned. The investigation, he was told by his superiors, was a fishing expedition, undoubtedly motivated by politics. He assumed the feds would ask a few questions about a grantee, someone who had gotten funding from the GOCCP, and then the whole thing would go away.

"I remember talking to the staff and telling them: 'There's been Democrats in office since (former Republican Gov. Spiro T.) Agnew,'" he recalled. "There's gonna be no change in parties, everybody's got career jobs here.

"See, I didn't face the reality of it at first," Amos continued. "I was oblivious to these kinds of political shenanigans. That's a big lesson: face reality."

As the probe dragged on and members of the administration began distancing themselves from him, Stephen realized he had misread the seriousness of the situation.

Worried and feeling alienated, he reached out to a small number of confidantes—I was honored to be one of them—to help keep his spirits up, strategize and crisis-lead during an incredibly difficult time. He also eschewed the standard advice about not saying anything to the media.

Instead, once a so-called "anonymous source" leaked to the press that a probe was underway, we invited the *Sun* and the other regional media outlets to go through the office files and see for themselves if there was any evidence of corruption.

The tactic worked brilliantly. Soon, editorials began appearing in the *Sun*, questioning DiBiagio's motives, one stating: "…it's tough to know right now if he is pursuing credible allegations of political corruption or has embarked on a fishing expedition."

The Ehrlich campaign, however, continued running political commercials that showed a prison cell door ominously slamming shut and a narrator asking if Maryland voters wanted another four years of a Democratic administration.

Subtle these ads weren't. No one could forget that the state crime office was under investigation.

Then, for a while, the investigation seemed to languish. Ehrlich won the election and took office in January. But with the *Sun* still asking to see evidence of corruption—if any existed—the case was resurrected.

The Washington Post, in the meantime, was pounding the GOCCP in a series of scathing articles hinting that Kathleen Kennedy Townsend and Stephen Amos were co-conspirators, misusing money that should have been going for crime prevention to pay for political tasks or non-existent staff.

The feds kept hammering away at Stephen, too, hoping he'd crack under the pressure and admit to wrongdoing.

"I could have taken a deal very early on," he said. "They offered me: 'Stephen, just give up Kathleen and you'll be free and clear of all this.' And I said: 'That ain't gonna happen. There's nothing here. You're going to have to show me what's a crime.'"

In the midst of all this, though he tried bravely not to show it, Stephen was spiraling downward. A talk with an old mentor at his previous job at the U.S. Department of Justice gave him an emotional lift and helped him change his attitude significantly.

"He said: 'You know, Stephen, you're gonna have to put on a game face here. You look like you just lost your whole family.' And he talked to me about compartmentalization: 'No matter what you're doing or what you're thinking, the staff will only define it through the reality of you as a leader.'"

While still torn-up emotionally, with his marriage crumbling and a child with a disability at home, Stephen somehow came to work every day and projected an upbeat manner. He knew the mission and integrity of the office was larger than himself, and that he needed to focus on that.

There were times I saw him being incredibly angry and frustrated behind closed doors. But he always managed to pull himself together before facing the staff, because he understood that his organization would follow his lead. The "Shadow of a Leader" concept—the concept that leaders can strongly influence the perceptions, behaviors and actions of those around them—was never more evident at the GOCCP.

Throughout his time there, Stephen worked with transparency and held regular meetings with his staff, briefing them on what he knew about the investigation, listening to their concerns and keeping their spirits up.

"I think that helped a lot because people saw I was upfront," he recalled. "I'm telling it like it is. As hard as that was, it gave me a sense of purpose every day."

Where weaker leaders might have bailed and quit, Stephen continued to hold himself and his staff accountable to advance the mission and get the work done.

But with Ehrlich sworn in as governor, the inevitable became reality. In the first week of February 2003, Stephen and six others at the agency were fired.

Stephen was not shocked by his dismissal, as government can be a very transient road at the highest levels. He continued to protest that he had done nothing wrong and that nothing improper had occurred at the agency. Nevertheless, a little over a year later, he was indicted on charges of misusing the GOCCP's grant money.

On March 29, 2004, on perhaps the lowest day of his life, he was arraigned in the U.S. District Court in Baltimore and plead not guilty to charges that he misappropriated $6.3 million in grant money, which the government alleged had paid for former Lt. Gov. Kathleen Kennedy Townsend's staff.

"That was a very traumatic day for me," Stephen recalled. "I remember so clearly standing in front of the judge and nobody there would (look) at my family. And I remember feeling so alone."

Yet it was also another defining event in the long, sad saga that had consumed him for so many months.

"I remember that as a time that I stood up in front of a federal judge in a federal courthouse and said 'I am not guilty and I don't accept these charges,'" he said proudly. "And it was one of those life-changing moments you'll never forget. Because I knew then that I was betting on the system and my integrity to carry me through the process versus what could have been a 30-year sentence."

He was not required to post bail that day and was released on his own recognizance. Yet on the ride home, a single terrifying thought played on a continuous loop in his head: *Who's gonna raise my son if I go to jail?*

"(Then) I remember going home and my son was still at the babysitter's," he said. "I crawled into bed with my suit on. And I remember waking up in the fetal position and thinking: '*My God, it can't get worse than this!*'"

For two more years, Stephen lived with the indictment hanging over his head, unable to land another job with his legal status in limbo. However, he was able to use his entrepreneurial spirit and drive some monies to his family through start-up business ventures. He was a very smart, resilient man.

But the toll on his personal life was enormous.

"I went on anti-depressants," he said. "My wife at the time became a severe alcoholic and dropped out of law school. She could not deal with it. We had been married 14 years and…they institutionalized her. I had a kid with a disability. And I was being threatened with 30 years in prison."

He was also forced to sell his house in Catonsville and five rental properties he owned to pay the bills. And after that money ran out, he borrowed from relatives to make ends meet.

"I remember I went to apply for a job at the National Organization on Fetal Alcohol Syndrome," he said. "This was a couple of months after I'd been fired. And I just started crying in the interview. I realized

I wasn't doing well."

It wasn't until January of 2005 that he received a call from his attorney, Gregg Bernstein, that began: "You're not gonna believe this…"

DiBiagio, Bernstein continued, had been fired. (Later it would be revealed the U.S. Attorney had allegedly been removed after a poor performance evaluation. According to *The Washington Post*, this came on the heels of a memo he'd sent in July of 2004 urging his prosecutors to obtain "Three Front-Page, White Collar/Public Corruption Indictments" before Nov. 6, four days after the presidential election.)

The charges against Stephen Amos had been dropped. They would be permanently expunged from his record.

"Justice has been served," *The Sun* editorialized, "but at a significant cost to Mr. Amos' reputation and livelihood."

Two years later, when Stephen was reimbursed for $193,194 in legal bills that he'd amassed defending himself from the charges, the newspaper would opine: "Anyone writing a text on abuse of power ought to include an entry on the…administration's handling of Stephen P. Amos."

In the end, though, what those of us who worked with Stephen during that trying period would remember was this: he was a warrior. He was the best kind of warrior, too, the kind you wanted in your foxhole. The kind who would never abandon his team or his mission.

No wonder Kathleen Kennedy Townsend, during her 60th birthday party a few years ago, made it a point to say to her former agency head: "You know, Stephen, there are obvious heroes, people who are out there who save a child or do this or that. But there are the silent heroes, the people who make the right decision every day. And they make that decision no matter what the cost is. That's the kind of leader you are."

KEY TAKEAWAYS

1. **Shed your ego.** After having worked at the local, state and

federal levels of government, I have seen a sense of institutional arrogance creep into decision-making at times. That is, "because we are who we are, we are right and can do what we want, when we want." This mindset and behavior is driven by people and can be changed by true leaders. While in these executive circles, I've often tried to make others pause and take a step back from their own egos and emotion to look at circumstances through the "customer's" lens vs. their own. In the Amos situation, there was no doubt in my mind that hundreds of thousands of dollars in public resources were irresponsibly spent to "prove" a crime had been committed, and to selfishly advance careers.

2. **Embrace reality.** One key lesson that Amos taught us was to face your reality quickly and stick to your principles along the way. In other words, don't pretend you aren't in grave danger because you don't feel the immediate pain—face reality and start managing the facts, quickly. A number of passengers on the Titanic knew they were in great danger before they felt the sharp, relentless pain of freezing water—many acted as quickly as possible. Pay attention to what your senses and instincts are telling you. Hoping bad situations will go away is never a sound tactic. In fact, I've never known a bad story to get better before it gets worse. Leaders must continue to predict and prepare for uncertainties even when life is going along just fine.

3. **Plan for the fork in the road.** I have worked with many clients under investigation for a variety of reasons, and most investigations were conducted by government agencies. During the course of the investigation/prosecution, there generally comes a time when a very important decision needs to be made—stick to your guns because you believe firmly in your principled innocence or strike a deal

to avoid protracted time, costs, freedom and sanity. This is an incredibly hard decision. Stephen Amos chose the former: to maintain his innocence no matter how long it took. Even though Stephen prevailed, he suffered mightily on the personal front. Ed Norris chose to strike a plea deal and do six months in jail. While he vehemently maintains his innocence, it seems as if Ed rebounded in his career a bit more quickly, as the process didn't drag on for many years. However, Ed is still left with a sense of loss because he can no longer do what he loved to do—catch bad guys. Think about and plan for decision day.

4. **Reinvent yourself, build marketplace value.** After a stint with the State Department in Afghanistan where Stephen helped many people, he is now, ironically, working for the U.S. Department of Justice, the very governmental body that once investigated him. While Stephen is doing fine today due to his own inner resilience, his ordeal came at a huge professional and personal toll. Be ready for the day when reinventing yourself is a must. The bottom line: make your decision about your future and don't look back—live life while looking through the windshield, not at what's behind you in the rear view mirror.

5. **Opportunists are everywhere.** I've seen it over and over again. When a leader is in trouble or wobbling due to crisis, few under him or her will maintain a strong sense of loyalty. Many others will remain silent or work covertly to push the leader out the door, hoping they can sit in the big chair one day soon. When you are embroiled in crisis, it can be a very lonely, thankless road—you become a perceived liability to others who are not willing to embrace the risk, even though you may be 100% in the right. The DNA of the opportunist is such that his or her loyalty is stalwart as long as it is politically expedient to do so

and ultimately advantageous to their careers. These are the wolves in sheep's clothing. Know who the wolves are and remove them from your camp—they are only there to facilitate your demise.

KEY CONCEPT.

The Coxswain

A CRISIS LEADERSHIP METAPHOR FROM THE ULTIMATE TEAM SPORT

In the stern of every four- and eight-oared rowing shell sits a person called the coxswain. This person is the brains behind the brawn: the on-water coach, the decision-maker, the leader. This person is responsible for race strategy, the safety of the crew and equipment, and ultimately, for ensuring that every rower knows exactly what to do and when to do it. The coxswain, not coincidentally, is the only person facing the direction in which the boat is moving: forward.

From the moment the crew puts hands on the boat, the coxswain is in charge. The crew places the highest level of trust in the coxswain, understanding the importance of their role in contributing to the whole. Every individual is incredibly important—the sum of everyone is exponentially greater than any one person. If one person, for one second, loses focus or misses a call, accidents happen, people get hurt, equipment can break, and races are lost.

Great coxwains, like crisis leaders, are part visionary, part strategist and part coach, and are always operating within a predictive mindset and factoring each nuance.

In any crisis, it only takes one action or incident, sometimes deceivingly minor, to derail an organization. At the moment a crisis occurs on the water, the leadership of the coxswain becomes even more important—the crew always knows whom to follow.

When a crisis occurs in your organization, do you have a coxswain? Does your crew know where to look for leadership guidance, strategy, tactics and recovery? Do you have someone that is "facing forward" and can see the big picture from the outside?

Imagine trying to move a 60-foot racing shell forward, while facing backwards, continuing to row, coordinating everyone else in your boat and constantly turning around to see if you're going to hit something. You can't do it. It's no different than trying to handle a crisis that is happening in your own organization without independent crisis leadership.

On the water, in an office or within our personal lives, something eventually happens that can throw the whole crew off balance, off course or threaten to sink the boat. In crisis management, what's important isn't whether or not the event that happens is large or small, but rather the ripple effect and how it is managed and contained.

Rowing is one of the most beautiful sports to watch. From a distance, a synchronized crew looks flawless, its minor mistakes invisible to those on shore. It is analogous to your company's reputation. Outsiders don't see or know every nuance or issue that occurs "in the boat." But before a crisis occurs and it affects reputation (how the outside world perceives your organization) the smartest thing you can do is assemble a confident, capable and highly experienced crisis leadership team that will get your crew rowing smoothly again, in the right direction.

13

When You're the Face of Crisis

You know them as spokespeople, press secretaries, public affairs reps, flacks and spin-doctors—that last term evoking the same warm and fuzzy feeling with the American public as "ambulance-chaser" and "wife-beater."

When a crisis engulfs their company, corporation or governmental agency, they stand in front of a bank of microphones and, with white-hot TV lights winking on and cameras rolling, they stare out into a sea of skeptical media faces and attempt to deliver a timely and coherent response on behalf of their employer.

I've learned from so many incredible communicators who are able to perform spectacularly under duress. It is an art, not a science. Like wine, spokespersons get better with age; there is no substitute for real experience. The best ones I know are obsessive about each syllable they utter, each piece of clothing they wear and each message point they deliver. They call reporters back, treat them all fairly and never, ever compromise their integrity. They understand what reporters need and make themselves relevant to those who have editorial control.

The best learn how to steer clear of organizational jargon, are detail-oriented and compassionately deliver the news in a conversational way that quickly and emotionally connects with those who consume their words. They are analytical, well-timed and process loads of information, almost instantaneously. And, they are never too high or too low—they have a steady hand under pressure no matter the gravity of the situation or tightness of deadline.

And, in the event they run into a "loose-cannon" reporter, they're able to manage the situation with the grace and humility of a verbal judo artist. With a Peyton Manning-like approach, the best are incredibly prepared, informed and always find a way to hone their craft. You want them on your team as they understand the big picture—it's what they do best—see the whole room.

It can be a thankless job. Yet, it is an absolutely vital one. As a spokesperson, you are the generally the most frequent ambassador of your company's brand. You are the reputational gate-keeper for your bosses and colleagues and stakeholders.

Bottom line: you better not screw it up, as you can lose your job with one syllable.

The pressure can be enormous, particularly with the 24-hour news cycle of today's world.

At no time was this lesson driven home to me more vividly than in the hot summer of 1997. At the tender age of 31, I was the newly-appointed public affairs director for the Baltimore Police Department when the sensational case of Charles M. Smothers II unfolded.

I was returning from a vacation in Ocean City on Maryland's Eastern Shore, when another of the department's spokespersons called.

The spokesperson had urgent news. There had been a police-involved shooting at Lexington Market, the historic indoor market downtown. An officer had shot a man with a knife. The scene was now extremely chaotic. Angry crowds were milling about.

"What should I do?" the spokesperson asked me in the midst of a brewing public safety crisis.

"Describe what limited amount of information you have to the news media—we have to have wiggle room, as facts will evolve with each minute," I answered. "Describe what happened as some type of interaction between the responding officers and the suspect. Say that detectives are going to comprehensively investigate and interview witnesses. We need to find out more before we can talk specifically about what happened."

My modus operandi and firm teaching point is to ask as many people as possible about the facts in an evolving case, knowing there could be varying accounts. Then, when the factual stars begin to align with consistency, you know you have a solid foundation with which to stand publicly. Credibility is key.

I was about to hang up when another thought occurred to me.

"Whatever you do," I said, "avoid action-oriented terms like 'lunge' or 'acted aggressively' to describe what the suspect did."

Again, what experience taught me is that very early on in police-shooting investigations, Public Information Officers, or PIOs, should never box themselves into a set of facts or circumstances that will almost always change.

I wasn't being some kind of schoolmarm-ish stickler for grammar here. I just knew we didn't have all the facts. Characterizing the encounter without knowing exactly what took place would be irresponsible. Plus, it could potentially blow up in our faces if we used what would later prove to be the wrong words.

The department spokesperson called back a short time later. She informed me that she'd done some preliminary interviews with the media. In a sheepish voice, she added: "I kind of got tripped up. And I used the word 'lunged.'"

Hearing this, I winced.

"OK," I said. "But let's not use it anymore. And we'll see what else transpires here."

The last thing I wanted to do was erode her confidence, as she had been the point of contact prior to me arriving back in town.

I still had one more day of vacation left, so my wife and I attended a friend's house party that evening. At some point, I learned that the officer involved in the shooting was Charles Smothers and that the man with the knife had been identified as James Quarles, now lying mortally-wounded in a hospital.

But the party would hardly be a festive, care-free time for me. At a few minutes before the 11 p.m. newscast, I received an urgent call from an assignment editor at WBAL-TV (the NBC affiliate) which was about to go live.

"Rob," he said, "we have video of the Lexington Market shooting."

I was stunned. For the first time in memory, we had a police shooting caught on tape. This was in the days before cell phones, when video was not the omnipresent phenomenon that it is today. (Later, I would learn that the station had paid a stringer fee of $500 to the man who had videotaped the incident with his camera.)

My first question to the WBAL editor, whom I had a relationship with, was direct: did he lunge?

The man with the knife—did he lunge at the officer as our spokesperson first reported?

"It looks like he didn't," the editor said. "It looks like he was shot for no reason."

Now I had a sinking feeling in my stomach. The TV station wanted a statement right away. They wanted to run it, along with their story of the shooting, at the top of their newscast just moments away.

Obviously, I had still not seen the video. I only knew what I had been told about the incident—I had to trust the judgement of a media member. And I knew what my instincts told me from my years on the streets as a patrol officer, which certainly helped now in my role as the department's chief spokesperson.

"This is a search for the truth," began the statement I quickly crafted. "The department encourages anyone who either witnessed or has information about the shooting to come forward and provide those facts to detectives to ensure that a very credible and thorough investigation occurs."

When the shooting story finally aired that night, everyone at the party gathered around the TV, watching intently. At the sight of the video, I nearly dropped my red Solo cup!

The assignment editor had been right: there was no lunge by the man with the knife. Instead, as he had seemingly attempted to put down the knife, the officer had fired his weapon. While I knew the suspect with the knife still posed a law enforcement threat, people at home watching would have a different point of view. Right or wrong, the video was certain to provoke a reaction.

It looked bad for Smothers. Bad for the police. Bad for Baltimore.

I looked at my wife and only half-jokingly said: "Vacation's over, pack it up!"

That night I called Clinton Coleman, press secretary to then-Mayor Kurt Schmoke, and briefed him on the incident.

"This is going to blow up," I warned. "It's not a small issue. We need to mobilize the faith and community-based leaders and all of our key ambassadors while urging the public to ask for patience—this is how riots start. We've seen that before. We've got a real flashpoint here. People are upset."

Over the course of the next few days, WBAL would run the videotape of the Smothers shooting some 200 times, according to sources at the station. The story gained more and more momentum.

The media was scrambling relentlessly to interview Smothers or his family. The family of the dead man, Quarles, was being similarly besieged. I knew reporters would soon start asking about police policies and procedures and begin questioning the personnel background of Smothers, looking for clues to his actions on that fateful day at the market.

In my briefing of the police department's command staff, I cautioned that a community firestorm could be averted only if citizens had confidence and trust that the department would conduct an honest, transparent investigation of the shooting and arrive at the right conclusion, whatever that turned out to be.

In the meantime, however, my mantra that "No bad story ever gets better before it gets worse," was again proven true. Because lo and behold, with every corner I turned on this case, it got worse.

First the department was hit with a bombshell revelation: Charles Smothers shouldn't have even been on the street in a police uniform at the time of the shooting.

Two years earlier, he had reportedly faced domestic violence charges for firing his service weapon at his ex-girlfriend and her new boyfriend, a Baltimore County police officer. Smothers had apparently claimed his weapon had discharged accidentally after it had fallen from his holster during a scuffle with the county cop. But the court hadn't believed that explanation.

Yet, even though he'd been convicted and sentenced to probation, as well as a mandatory administrative hearing, Smothers had somehow been allowed to keep his badge and gun and return to the force, directly contravening the department's policies on officer domestic-abuse cases.

So now the question internally became: do we tell the news media all of this?

A lot of the commanders said no. But my position was: we should absolutely give the details to the media.

I felt this way because another of my mantras is this: "always shovel shit by the shovel, not by the teaspoon." Meaning: get all the bad news out right away. Don't let it come out in dribs and drabs, at which point it looks like you're lying, or at the very least, covering-up or stone-walling the investigation.

Yes, the department letting Smothers return to the street was terribly embarrassing. Yes, someone had made an egregious mistake. But we could find out how that had happened later. Whoever had screwed up could be disciplined, if warranted. And we could ensure that something like that never happened again.

But right now, we were more concerned about the reputation of the department and the need to do everything possible to quell any brewing unrest over the shooting while being sensitive to the family who just lost a loved one. We needed the public to know we were looking into the case with the utmost transparency, honesty and integrity.

Fortunately, my commander teammates listened to me. We released everything we knew about Smothers' crime. Predictably, it created a huge media firestorm.

As I was quickly reminded, dealing with crisis is exhausting. It's a 24-hour-a-day job, and the search for more details never stops. By now, the story of the rogue Baltimore cop who probably shouldn't have ever been allowed back on the street—and who'd gunned down a man who appeared to be surrendering his weapon—had gone international.

The media were playing hardball with the story, too. There were many questions, but few answers. Investigations take time, but everyone wants answers yesterday.

A day later, as I worked in my office on the first floor of police headquarters, the door was suddenly flung open. I looked up and there was a light shining in my face, a TV camera rolling and someone holding a big fuzzy boom mike above my head.

A woman with a foreign accent barked: "We're looking for Robert *Vine*-holt!"

The reporter and her camera crew were from "Hard Copy," the tabloid news show that was often paired with "Entertainment Tonight" back then. They had ambushed me for comments on the Smothers' mess.

When I told the reporter that I'd be more than happy to do the interview, but that I needed a few moments to gather my thoughts and get ready, she said: "OK, but we're not leaving until you talk to us."

When I finally did the interview a half-hour later, the first question was this: "Aren't you *embarrassed* to be associated with a police department like this?"

You'll be shocked to know the questions went downhill from

there. I was prepared for the haymaker out of the gate—in this profession, that's not unusual at all.

The media circus got worse. When reporters couldn't find Smothers to get his side of the story, they staked out his mother's house. One particularly aggressive reporter knocked on the door and quickly got into an argument with the mom, who was understandably upset that her son was now receiving death threats and being hounded by reporters.

The next time a reporter knocked, the woman who answered the door and threw what was initially thought to be a lye mixture in the reporter's face. The reporter went down and was rushed by ambulance to a local hospital. Luckily, she suffered no permanent damage. I felt sorry for the reporter, one of the nicest in town. She had simply fallen victim to a situation best described by the old truism: "The one who stirs the hornet's nest is rarely the one who gets stung."

After that incident, I gathered the media, repeated that tensions were high and recommended they stay away from the mother's house. "The next thing that could happen might involve gunshots," I told them.

Yet in the end, the department's strategy of transparency and communicating openly with those in the community who were most upset paid off.

No riots or civil unrest broke out in Baltimore in the wake of the Smothers shooting, despite it being on video. People took a step back. Peace prevailed. I really began to appreciate the critical role a public affairs director for a big-city police department could play for the men and women in blue and the jurisdictions they serve, when crisis occurs.

There would be many other difficult times when I would be out front as the voice and face of the Baltimore PD, learning all the other skills of an effective public affairs director.

When an officer was killed in a traffic accident, and days later another officer went down in a helicopter crash, I went from the grave site of a police funeral to the University of Maryland Medical Center's Shock Trauma unit, where the second officer was clinging to life. (He would die shortly after.)

At a hastily-called news conference that day, Jennifer Gilbert, a veteran reporter for FOX-45, said: "Rob, this is unimaginable. Can you describe the feeling of the department right now?"

What an immense responsibility that was!

To be asked, off the top of your head, to define how 3,000 or 4,000 men and women would feel in the wake of such a devastating loss. It was a question I wish I never had to answer—it was the closest I ever came to shedding tears on camera. All I could think about were the families of the officers and the horrible news they'd just received. I quickly snapped out of it, as many depended on me to capture the moment, not cry on camera.

Yet I would be asked to do something similar many times, to provide perspective to people who didn't live in the police world or understand life on the street, to bridge the gap between the tragic reality of whatever crisis was occurring and people's perceptions of it. That's what an effective public affairs director can do: take the complex or unbelievable and make it easily consumable for others to understand, no matter how grim.

When police Lt. Owen Sweeny was shot through a door and killed just months before his retirement; when a two-year-old named Asia Nichols was shot in the head by her father, who was in the midst of a domestic dispute; when Walter E. Loch, a retired Johns Hopkins physician, and his wife, Mary, were beaten to death with a baseball bat as they slept in their home (their grandson would eventually confess to the crime)—in all of those senseless, high-profile crimes, I was the face delivering horrific news to the public.

I had to deliver it in a credible, professional, articulate way, while also being the voice of reason and humanizing the events so people not only understood the facts, but also how it impacted the community within the context of larger public policy discussions and debates.

A good spokesperson, I learned, is not just someone who regurgitates facts. It's someone who pays attention in his or her remarks to delivery, cadence and voice inflection—someone who can think on his or her feet, who can take something technical and break it down so that the message is understood. In short, they tell a story in the most conversational of tones.

If the story is understood, truly understood no matter how painful or joyful the news, then the spokesperson has done their job.

KEY TAKEAWAYS

1. **Never erode your integrity.** Misinformation breeds distrust. As a spokesperson there is, at times, an immense pressure to make your organization look good. Do not cave in to others who would like you to lie, distort the truth or leave vital facts behind which alter messaging and perception—this is tantamount to a lie. Once lost, you will never fully restore your integrity.

2. **Be relevant.** As the art of press relations evolves within a changing worldwide media landscape, I hear about more and more spokespeople not returning reporter calls, delaying the release of information, and simply refusing to feed the "media monster." However, the "monster" will eat! And as long as the "monster" eats, media reps will need access and information in order to tell their stories effectively. If you, as a press contact, choose to stick your head in the sand and not respond, you make yourself quickly irrelevant and ineffective. As an executive who depends on the advice of your communications expert, understand this principle and make yourself available. Remember the mantra, "If you don't tell your story, someone else will. And, when someone else tells your story, it certainly won't be the story you want told."

3. **Know the facts.** A common mistake of many who speak

publicly is not fully preparing and gaining a sound understanding of the facts before the interview. Too many times,
I have seen professionals jump out on camera with either
no substantive information to deliver or relying solely on
the old fallbacks "I can't comment on that" or "I don't
have that information." This drives consumers of the
news berserk. Not knowing the facts or relying on the
"no comment" phrase will quickly make you irrelevant to
everyone—it is unacceptable. A spokesperson is expected
to—and paid to—know the facts. While you may feel you
have done your job by surviving the interview or press
conference, you have done nothing to inform the audience and lend the perspective so sorely needed during life's
most critical times. Sometimes spokespeople cave into
media requests ("I just need something on camera"), organizational pressure or self-imposed deadlines. Bottom line:
if you decide to step up to the podium, have something
important to say!

4. **Be predictive.** When preparing to go on camera or prepping another, be certain to plan for every question and
eventuality. There is often a tendency for folks to want
to go on camera without fully preparing, because they are
used to speaking publicly or know the organization very
well—chief executives are good for this. Push back and
demand ample preparation. List questions, answers, fol-
low-ups and counters—it is a mental chess game. Train on
camera, relentlessly. Failing to plan is planning to fail. An
eight to fifteen second sound bite can ruin your career—
just ask BP's former chief executive Tony Hayward, who
recklessly uttered in 2010 "I want my life back" after an
explosion and one of the world's most damaging oil spills
killed 11 people and spilled some 4.9 million barrels of oil
into the Gulf of Mexico. Don't wing it, prepare for every

interview no matter how mundane or harmless it may seem.

5. **Build relationships with those who have editorial control.** Know those who tell your story. I want to get the benefit of the doubt when the reporter tells his or her story—I don't want an unfair advantage, simply balance. Gather intelligence from reporters and news organizations—ask them what angle they plan to take with their story. Yes, they are under no obligation to tell you. But you'd be amazed at what they *will* tell you, particularly if there is an existing relationship or future mutual need.

6. **Video doesn't tell the whole story.** In the Smothers case, the video account of what happened did not tell many things: what each party said, body language from all angles, what transpired before and after the footage. In today's digital world, everyone is a journalist with an opinion. More is recorded and shared than at any other point in history. Make no mistake about it, the emergence of video has changed all professions. But be very careful when making a judgment or decision based solely on what video has to offer. There are many more aggravating and mitigating circumstances to consider. Treat video for what it is: another tool in the search for the truth.

KEY CONCEPT

Media Relations Quick Tips

Develop and articulate messages:

Know what you want your audience to know.

Be the expert—know your subject matter.

Be clear and concise.

Be passionate, focused and disciplined.

Repetition creates awareness.

Bridge to your core messages routinely.

Anticipate audience reaction to messages.

Test core messages with trusted stakeholders.

Always:

Maintain eye contact with the interviewer.

Limit facial, hand and body movement.

Remember: you are never "off the record."

Know and understand the facts.

Be decisive and truthful.

Know and commit to stakeholders.

Illustrate leadership.

Provide perspective.

Be empathetic and listen.

Identify advocates and use one voice.

Correct misinformation.

Operate in a controlled setting.

Establish your pace.

Be professional and respectful.

Be conversational.

Practice, practice, practice.

Never:

Speculate.

Be defensive.

Say "no comment."

Repeat a negative.

Let misinformation stand as fact.

Run away or cover camera lens.

Lie.

14

Data Breach: Today's Silent Digital Danger

As I've preached to CEO's for years, a crisis can come from anywhere and hit at any time.

Mark Curtis first felt the full impact of his company's crisis amid the spectacular setting of Jackson Hole, Wyoming, the popular vacation resort ringed by the regal Teton Mountains that tower over lush green forests and alpine meadows dotted with wildflowers and feeding elk.

Curtis is one of the founders of Splash Car Wash, a 35-year-old company with 19 locations in Connecticut and New York that employs over 500 workers.

In the summer of 2014, he attended a key executive retreat for the International Car Wash Association at a hotel in Jackson Hole. I happened to be there as a featured speaker and facilitator on leadership, strategy and communications.

During one of the breaks, I saw Mark engaged in an animated conversation on his cell phone. When he hung up, he approached me with a worried look.

"Hey," he said, "I may need your help. We may have a data breach."

Initially, Splash officials had hoped the problem was confined to one location, and that it was related to employee theft rather than a breach.

But by the time Mark got off the phone that morning and huddled with me, the news was far grimmer: the company had a major data breach on its hands. Thousands of its credit-card-paying customers were potentially affected.

"We had been hacked," Curtis recalled, "hacked by people similar to or the same as the ones that had hacked Target and other big companies. Essentially what (the hackers) had done is, they had infiltrated our system to the extent they could read a credit card from the swipe on a cash register before it was encrypted and then sent through the telephone wire to the company to get payment.

"It was as if they had set up a skimmer on our POS," he continued, referring to the point of sale system, or the company's cash registers. "You know how (the cashier) runs the card down the slot? Well, that immediately goes into a program that's encrypted, and then that information is sent out so nobody can read it, including us. That ensures there can't be internal theft."

The hackers would then intercept the credit card info, including the card number and expiration date. And that information would be sold to people that could produce fake credit cards that are used to quickly buy gift cards to be converted into cash.

The U.S. Secret Service was already investigating Splash Car Wash's nightmare. Data breaches at businesses throughout the country were becoming more and more frequent, and their effects could be devastating.

A year earlier, Target Corporation had suffered a massive breach of its computer systems that resulted in the compromising of 40 million credit and debit card accounts. The hackers also came away with a ton of personal information, including names and addresses of some 70 million people who had shopped at the retail chain.

In September of 2014, home improvement retailer Home Depot would suffer a similar breach that exposed some 56 million credit cards and countless email addresses. Two months later, Sony Pictures Entertainment would report that its computer system had been infiltrated, the hackers gaining access to "mountains" of sensitive data and "stolen documents."

(This would include embarrassing personal emails purportedly exchanged by Amy Pascal, the head of Sony Pictures, and producer Scott Rudin, that contained racially-insensitive jokes about President Barack Obama's taste in movies.)

For a far smaller company like Splash Car Wash, having its computer system hacked can be even more crippling.

"The biggest concern, obviously, is people's reaction to a data breach," Mark said. "The initial reaction is that somehow the company has either stolen the money, is complicit in the theft, or is negligent in the way they handled the customers' information.

"In defense of Home Depot, Target and the rest of us who have fallen into this (predicament), nothing could be further from the truth."

My advice to Mark and his executive team was to immediately control the rules of engagement. That is, you take the bull by the horns, get in front of the information curve and follow the Resilient Moment Communications model in hybrid fashion—tell people what happened, why it happened, who's responsible, what the short- and long-term ramifications are, what customers need to do next, and what you're doing to prevent something like this from happening in the future.

Within 24 hours of my initial conversations with Mark, Splash sent emails to the 300,000 customers on its internal email list explaining the situation and the fixes being put in place.

The emails also urged customers to review their credit card statements if they did business with Splash that spring. Finally, the messages apologized profusely for the inconvenience and instructed customers with further questions or concerns to call a special 800 phone number the company had set up.

Somehow, at least one of the emails was also forwarded to the local Connecticut and New York newspapers. While Splash had been on the verge of issuing an official press release, the local papers quoted the emails almost verbatim, essentially getting the word about the hacking out to that many more customers not on the company's email list. This definitely worked in our favor. Personally, I'd much rather hear bad news about a data breach from a company I patronize, rather than the media.

The result of all this transparency and timely advice was "fantastic," Mark said. "I think we received 200 phone calls and 100 emails. And I'm going to tell you that 95 percent of them were either commendations for how we were handling the problem or a simple question like 'OK, what should I do?'

"Maybe 10 of all those calls and emails were ridiculous, like 'I can't believe you're doing this to me, you're screwing me!' Of course, we answered 'No, we're not, we didn't do this, it wasn't our intent, we do take precautions and yadda, yadda, yadda.'

"You're always going to get that fringe element. What amazed me was the number of people saying 'We really appreciate you taking the responsibility and getting out front of this and letting us know what's happening.'"

Splash Car Wash immediately ceased using its POS machines and went back to using the old ZON series terminals, where the customer's card was swiped, the amount of the sale was recorded manually, and was not connected to the cash register.

It was an antiquated system that required duplicate work for the cashiers at each location. But until the data breach could be permanently repaired, it was the safest option for Splash's customers.

Mark and his executive team, as well as the head of Splash's human resource training, also began conducting regular scripted conference calls with each of the cashiers to let them know what to expect of the new system and how to respond to customers' questions. As a result of all these steps, Splash was able to weather the data breach and retain the confidence of its customer base. Trust is all anyone has in today's global marketplace.

"In retrospect, it really turned out incredibly well," Mark said. "There might have been a momentary lull in (business)—maybe for a day or so. We thought it was going to be far more impactful."

But by the fifth day after notifying their customers of the problem, Splash executives were fairly confident that they had a handle on the breach and its ripple effects.

"The best thing we did," Mark told me, "was to take your advice and get out in front of the problem. Rather than playing defense, go on offense. Admit you have a problem, say what you're doing to fix it, apologize for the problem and say why it won't happen again.

"As the leader of a company," he added, "my other advice would be to not stick your head in the sand and hope the problem goes away. (Problems) have a tendency to grow bigger and more problematic if you don't address them. And I know people might think 'If we don't talk about it, don't say anything…' But if it's a real problem, it's so much better to (address) it."

To me, the favorable ending to Splash's data breach issue was really a testament to Mark Curtis' leadership. I say that because following our initial conversation in Jackson Hole on how to handle the problem, Mark had stepped into unfamiliar territory.

He had to trust that my Fallston Group team and I knew what we were doing. He had to believe this enough to follow my advice, despite the fact that others on his executive team might have had different opinions on how to deal with the crisis.

I give him a lot of credit. He was very proactive. He took a strong leadership stance and controlled the story.

He had the foresight to realize that putting your hand up and saying, "We've got an issue," is a long-term strategy that's important to the viability of a business. Because now, customers know that if another issue comes up in the future, he's going to handle it openly, directly and with integrity.

KEY TAKEAWAYS

1. **Define the rules of engagement.** The speed at which information is disseminated and the pace at which leaders must operate is incredible. Particularly for large organizations like Target and Home Depot, once the legal side of the corporation and other key decision-makers get involved, decision-making and reaction time slows at the highest levels. Define the rules of engagement, hence your message. People want leadership and direction, not vacillating decision-making when every moment counts.

2. **Be first.** Don't let others break the bad news for you... do it yourself, on your terms with precision and accuracy. Again, use the Resilient Communications Model to satisfy the overwhelming number of questions that people will have. Make certain there is a call to action.

3. **Digital is the new battlefield, protect yourself.** According to the Institute for Crisis Management (2015), there was a 30 percent jump in reported data breach incidents in 2014 in the U.S. alone. The average hacker is in your computer network on the order of nine months before he or she is even detected. Think about it this way: when your neighborhood is being cased by a burglar, he takes a lot of time to study the ingress and egress routes, when the residents come and go, their behavioral patterns, and so on. The burglar is waiting for the right time to strike. Hackers do the same thing. The only difference is, they do it digitally. Whether by implementing end-user data security awareness training, intrusion detection systems, vulnerability testing or engaging employee behavior monitoring programs, be certain to spend the resources to protect your data. In the worst case scenarios where a breach has occurred, ensure your organization has an executable data

breach crisis plan in place where all know exactly what to do from both a technical and executive standpoint. One of life's most basic needs for human beings is to feel safe—digital safety is no exception. As many in the business say, there are two types of organizations: those who have been hacked and those who don't know it yet!

4. **Be relevant, address social media complaints head-on.** Respond authentically—never use an alias or pose as someone you are not. Converse on the same social media platform where the conversation is occurring. Be thankful, polite, respectful and solution-based. Tell customers how you are going to address their concerns. Take it off-line when possible—human interaction is key. Reiterate that the organization always strives for excellence. Highlight your company's strengths, never a competitor's weakness. Evaluate what you can do to repair the relationship quickly. Validate the complaint. Surveys show when a negative review is acknowledged in a human way, many original posters will either change their post or remove the negative comment. Bottom line, again: "If you don't tell you story, someone else will. And when someone else tells your story, it certainly won't be the story you want told."

KEY CONCEPT

The 15/70/15 Paradigm

In almost every crisis I've handled, I've found the 15/70/15 Paradigm holds true, with a few percentage point shift either way. During a crisis, if you metaphorically punched 15 percent of your most loyal stakeholders square in the nose, it would be the best punch in the nose they've ever received. They will support and have an affinity for you and your brand no matter what, as long as you did not do something terribly egregious by any moral or human standard.

The next 15 percent will be offended if you hand them a bar of gold or a winning lottery ticket in the wrong manner. That is, nothing you can say or do will appease or sway them from a negative position or stance, even though your crisis management goal is to bring them from negative to neutral. In fact, most outspoken, passionate critics or organizations fall into this category. For instance, no matter how good an amenity or development project may be for a community, ardent support will never come from anti-growth people or land preservationist groups. In fact, they will be working against you in an emotional, mobilized fashion.

The real reputational battleground, however, is the 70 percent in between the positive and negative opinions. You are fighting for their support—their opinions can be influenced. By support, I mean bringing their opinions or perceptions from negative to neutral or neutral to positive about a particular issue. This is a really important concept, as people buried in controversy must understand they will almost never win unanimous support. But that doesn't mean there isn't a "win" to strive for. The "win" will ultimately be defined in many unique ways, depending on the business or life goals of those embroiled or the teams that support them.

15

Vulgar, Visual then Viral

While traveling near New York City on a cold March Sunday afternoon, my iPhone began ringing incessantly. Soon, text messages began popping at an alarming rate, and my email account was flooded with urgent messages.

Such message clusters are generally not from folks who want to chit-chat and ask how your day is going.

After calling various sources, I learned five players on the University of Maryland, Baltimore County (UMBC) women's lacrosse team had been suspended, accused of making threats on social media to harm—and kill—some of their freshmen teammates.

The *Baltimore Post-Examiner*, a news website, had run a story about the suspensions, complete with images of the alarming texts that had been sent on GroupMe, a messaging app that bills itself as "a private chat room for your small group."

Except what these young women posted definitely hadn't remained private.

Instead, one of the freshmen players had discovered the threatening texts. Soon, the freshmen players notified their parents and coaches, who then went to the university's athletic director. Shortly after, the story had been leaked to the *Post-Examiner* site.

Other media outlets, including Baltimore's major daily newspaper, the *Sun*, and various national news outlets, were also looking into the story. And now, the very emotional parents of one of the suspended players were asking me for help in dealing with the growing media firestorm that was portraying their daughter in an unflattering light, and threatening to permanently damage her reputation, perhaps even well after her college playing days had ended.

After quickly arriving back in Baltimore, I arranged for a conference call with the parents of all five young women. Soon a different story began to emerge—one far more nuanced than the already breathless media coverage would suggest.

Basically, all of the suspended players—a senior, junior and three sophomores—had become extremely frustrated with the Retrievers' coaches. The young women felt the coaches were playing favorites and were engaged in the uneven treatment of players. And this, the older players felt, was because of a personal grudge one particular coach held against them. (Those of us that have been around youth sports understand one very important fact: amateur sports bring out the very best and worst in people. I learned this quickly in my nearly two decades of coaching various sports teams.)

So the older players had vented their gripes on what they thought was a private digital platform.

In the full flower of youth, they had exchanged such hyperbolic postings as: "I tried to fucking swipe that bitch's head off" and "I'm only aiming for her fucking shins and then I'll aim for her fucking head and hair" and "Take down the coaches. Kill the freshmen."

"A lot of dumb things were said," admitted Jack Milani, the father of one of the sophomore suspended players. "It was a bitch session that they thought was private."

After all, it was the way young people today often communicate—digitally.

Yet, now the suspended women and their families felt helpless and isolated in the face of the national media onslaught. In fact, by now the story had gone international.

ABC's "Good Morning America" was particularly relentless in bringing the story to its viewers, repeatedly calling the bar that Milani co-owns in suburban Baltimore and pressuring employees for his cell number. When that didn't work, the show's producers even called his wife's parents. Clearly, each of the young women caught up in the controversy had become the "villainess" so central to great story-telling.

The families of the suspended players were also frustrated at what they saw as the school's maddening inability to understand that their daughters were just venting harmlessly, and that none of their dark mutterings on social media should have been taken seriously. In fact, according to Milani the university's Student Affairs Department interviewed each scrutinized student and deemed each not to be a threat to the school. Milani adds that as a result of the university's probe, the students never missed a day of class.

"Common sense was thrown out the window after the first couple of days," Jack Milani said. "If it was me, I would have suspended these girls for a while, made them apologize maybe for the third or fourth time."

"Then I'd have brought them back and said: 'OK, we're gonna make this an educational (tool)…that will prevent other kids from going through this.'"

Similarly, another parent was worried that the suspended players' lives would be ruined forever and that they'd never be able to play lacrosse again or land a decent job anywhere. After all, it's incredibly hard to outrun a Google search.

After analyzing all of the facts, it was clear to me that there was no way around the vulgarity and tone that the suspended players had used on a digital messaging application.

At a different point in time, maybe 20 years ago, their words might have been laughed off. Or they might have been equated to the macho, exaggerated threats routinely heard in football, where saying, "When they come across the middle, we're gonna take their heads off," doesn't even raise an eyebrow.

But in today's world, when such words are delivered via digital media, in writing that fairly drips with anger and frustration, they take on a more sinister tone, particularly when there is no sense of voice inflection or perspective.

At this point, the suspended players were also being blasted on social media.

They had become harassers in the eyes of many. They had become bullies. And, potentially, they had become young women who might carry out an assault.

School-based assaults (verbal or physical) are a very serious matter in today's world. No amount of "I didn't really mean it" will lead to an immediate forgive-and-forget scenario. Not only were the playing days of the women in jeopardy, so was their student-athlete status.

The first order of business, I told the parents of the suspended players, was to humanize their daughters in the eyes of their aggrieved teammates, UMBC stakeholders, and the traditional and digital news media. The "court of public opinion" was in full deliberation mode and rendering verdicts about the student athletes' behavior by the second.

These were young, otherwise-accomplished women who had made a terrible mistake. They hadn't intended to hurt anyone. They had let their emotions get the best of them. That needed to be conveyed in the form of a sober, heart-felt apology. There was no acceptable explanation; what the girls had communicated was wrong and deplorable by every standard.

So, on behalf of four of the suspended players (the fifth opted not to be included), I quickly issued a statement to all members of the local, national and international news media that said, in part:

"First and foremost, our hurtful, destructive words and tone are absolutely inexcusable on many levels. Our stance was utterly inappropriate and we are deeply sorry to the many we negatively impacted, particularly our hard-working teammates who deserve much better.

"Words cannot express our sense of regret and disappointment in ourselves. We know that everyone deserves to be treated with the utmost dignity and respect—we let our emotions get the best of us over time and we failed…Our goal is to humbly work through this difficult situation with hopes of achieving an outcome that makes the best long-term sense for all involved."

While I don't normally speak publicly for clients for a variety of reasons, I did do interviews with the *Sun*, The Associated Press and several TV stations in the following days. I felt the players were too emotional to speak for themselves at this point and the parents were, in many cases, more upset than the players. However, the humanization effort couldn't stop with an issued apology—we had to bring their heartfelt sorrow to life.

In each interview, I attempted to lend some perspective to the story, to make sure people knew how contrite the young women were, and that they had fired-off the damning messages out of frustration, not because of any inherent mean-spiritedness. I felt well-equipped to do this as an experienced interviewee, father and coach. I understood the dynamic completely.

Concurrently, I was also communicating with UMBC officials as the parents claimed they had no luck with return phone calls. The school, of course, wanted this whole scandal to go away quickly. Instead, it was dragging on and on. How could we balance the interests of the university, the team and most importantly, the young women I now represented? I had worked in government long enough to know that decision-making at a bureaucratic level was never quick; in fact, once the attorneys get involved, they seem to drive most decisions at a snail's pace. While they serve an incredibly important purpose, attorneys are generally very risk adverse.

My goal was to accelerate this issue through the news cycle as quickly as possible. I needed to find a point of leverage to get the university to listen and act quickly. I made contact with and encouraged school officials to meet with the suspended players and their families—and then with the entire team and family members—in an attempt to bring people together and establish a sense of transparency and communication. It was clear the team dynamic was in shambles and the coaches or athletic department couldn't do it on its own. The university's executive team needed to be involved at the highest levels and show true leadership.

I knew the suspended players and parents were growing more desperate and wanted to hold their own press conference to talk about the team, its coaches and what led the young women to the point of boiling over. They wanted to defend themselves and go on the offensive because their own institution wasn't supporting them.

If that happened, no one knew what kind of hurtful, inflammatory rhetoric would come out. It was my sense the university would be on its heels if the players moved to tell all, from their own perspective and in their own words.

By now, another element had been introduced: the "Dr. Phil" show was calling, wanting all five players to appear to tell their story. This was intriguing—we were at the height of the media storm and Dr. Phil McGraw's popular show provided an international therapeutic platform for my clients. With each minute of university indecision, the option became more appealing on many strategic levels.

One key benefit of the Dr. Phil show was the SEO (Search Engine Optimization) implications and the need to digitally balance the story for future Internet articles. Once this ordeal was over and the players sought professional careers, we didn't want one-sided stories to be first and foremost when a suspended player's name was searched on the Web. Dr. Phil was willing to fly the players to a number of different places in the country to tell their story, which meant I had a chit in the balance to use in talks with the school.

I continued to push and finally the university agreed to facilitate a closed, evening meeting among all parents and players so everyone could be heard and validated. My goal was to bring the temperature of the crisis down and slow the emotional decision-making. My clients needed to know they had the ear of the university officials who could make decisions and act in everyone's interest.

In the end, the media circus came to town and left quickly after the issued public apology and interviews. (We gave the media no access to the suspended players or their parents, even though we had strategies in place should the media covertly try to entrap a student or family member.)

Meanwhile, the university continued to investigate my clients' cases—albeit with a little more external pressure. While it was understandable that a review of this magnitude takes time, my clients' athletic and academic lives hung in the balance, with little clarity as to their ultimate fate.

I encouraged the university to be firm, fair and timely. In the end, the suspended players all exercised different options. Some were reinstated, some transferred and some hung up their spikes and called it a career. All of us are guilty of speaking our minds without thinking at times, but the ability to digitally broadcast our unfiltered thoughts—for a permanent record—can be very dangerous. Helping students develop sound conflict resolution strategies to solidify the team culture instead of engaging in destructive activity would benefit many, at all levels of amateur sports.

KEY TAKEAWAYS

1. **Make a decision.** Theodore Roosevelt said it best, "In any moment of decision, the best thing you can do is the right thing, the next best thing is the wrong thing, and the worst thing you can do is nothing." The same can be said when it comes to crisis planning, management and recovery. It was clear this event caught UMBC leadership off-guard and they did not have a crisis management policy or protocol to follow. In fact, they were initially paralyzed by the facts and scrambling due to a lack of leadership direction and decision-making. One of the biggest leadership mistakes is a failure to plan, hence act. Without an executable crisis

plan and crisis team to decision-make, organizations are handicapped and blindsided when adversity strikes—no decision is a decision. A key hallmark of any great leader is the ability to make a decision when many others are frozen and depending on someone else for guidance.

2. **Be predictive and have a crisis plan.** Organizations must be predictive in nature and create organizational muscle memory through extensive assessment, policy development and training. Seriously evaluate each company-based and industry threat. Leaders and their reporting streams must be empowered to make decisions during life's most critical times, even in the absence of key executives. Establish a crisis team and plan. The crisis plan should include the creation of an extended team within the institution to mobilize during crisis, based on tested policies and training.

3. **Author a digital or new media policy.** Every organization, particularly collegiate athletic programs where young people are thrust onto a larger life stage for the very first time, should have a digital media policy and ensure that each employee or team member undergoes social and digital media training. Everyone in today's world must understand the power of and consequences that accompany the use of social media and new technology. It seems every misdeed is caught on an audio or video file waiting to be shared with the world. Understand that dynamic.

4. **There is no such thing as a private digital transmission.** All people must understand that in today's world, everyone who participates has two reputations—in-person and digital. Both are fragile, but digital reputation is the hardest to manage because thoughts and feelings are communicated so impulsively and quickly. If it's vulgar and visual, it's viral. Think before you post—your future depends on it!

5. **Know your point of leverage.** Understanding the motives of all parties involved in crisis will drive outcomes. This sounds simple, but knowing the university's points of pain (what they didn't want to happen) helped me initially put my clients in a more leveraged position. For example, if the university continued to ignore my clients, the likelihood of them going public and exposing more team issues would rise, possibly causing significant embarrassment for the school. Use your points of leverage. My goal wasn't to harm the school, but to coach the university into crisis-leading in a timely manner that resolved the situation and created a long-term win-win for everyone concerned.

16

The Smoldering Sex Scandal

The Reisterstown Volunteer Fire Company, a large, active unit in the northwest suburbs of Baltimore, is rarely a place of intrigue.

Most days, the focus is on preparation, training and equipment maintenance, the hum-drum yet satisfying routine between those adrenalized moments when firefighters put their lives on the line responding to catastrophic medical emergencies or rolling up to a roaring inferno.

But all that changed in March of 2015.

On a sunny afternoon, the Reisterstown Company was rocked by a bombshell: county police were investigating allegations of sexual misconduct involving at least two male firefighters and at least one female firefighter.

The news quickly leaked. Within hours, the media descended on the company's firehouse. TV cameras doing live shots were set up on the sidewalk outside. Reporters knocked on the firehouse door and called incessantly, demanding further information.

"This is a serious investigation," a police spokesperson told *The Baltimore Sun* newspaper.

Forty-eight hours later, two more male firefighters were linked to the investigation. But the police declined to describe the nature of the allegations, leaving many to assume the worst. And as the days went by with no further police clarification about the criminal probe, rumors and innuendo swept through the venerable company, which was founded in 1915 and listed 170 members (80-100 active).

Fortunately, in president James (J.P) Snyder, a calm, unassuming 41-year-old, the company had a leader who was proactive, and not reactive.

Snyder was serving his second term as president. (He had been the vice president a year before that and president the six previous years.) Wholly unschooled in how to react to a possible sex scandal that threatened enormous reputational damage to the fire company, he quickly realized he needed a professional crisis leadership group and reached out to our team.

"When the media got involved," Snyder said, "that (was) an aspect that we, as volunteers, never had to deal with before. We were overwhelmed."

I, along with my colleague, Josie Hankey, met with J.P. and the fire company's executive board in an emergency meeting the Saturday morning after he called.

Fallston Group's goal was to thoroughly understand the facts of the case, so we could assist the fire company from a leadership, strategy and communications standpoint. Based on the information we had, the company needed to know what strategic steps to take next.

Complicating things, rumors were flying and there were human resource issues in play. Since there was an ongoing criminal investigation, we needed to be respectful of the integrity of that, too. And we had to make sure the right messaging was out there in the court of public opinion.

With reporters buzzing around and TV cameras rolling outside the firehouse, the media was basically telling the company's story about the investigation and any alleged sexual misconduct.

But no one from the fire company was saying anything. Their message—their side of the story—wasn't being told at all. Once again, the all-important mantra of Fallston Group had come into play: If you don't tell your story, someone else will. And when someone else tells your story, it certainly won't be the story you want told.

That first meeting with J.P. and the 12 members of the fire company's executive board lasted eight hours.

In order to instill a sense of confidence that the company was taking the matter seriously, cooperating with the investigation and making sure it would be holding its members accountable, we prepared a statement on behalf of the fire company and distributed it to the media.

It was important for J.P. to quickly acknowledge an investigation was taking place, and to encourage anyone who had information about the matter to come forward and cooperate with investigators.

We worked hard on scripting and messaging, identifying primary and secondary spokespeople so that if the media called, the calls were passed along to the right person for comment. We even did on-camera media training with the fire chief.

We wanted people inside and outside the firehouse—the internal and external stakeholders—to know that the search for the truth in this matter was on.

Again, J.P. showed true leadership skills from the onset of the crisis.

He didn't sit back and wait for the criminal investigation to conclude before taking action internally. The scandal had been smoldering for a while; although J.P. hadn't heard them, whispers of untoward sexual behavior involving firefighters had been around for almost a year.

It was clearly time to act. And J.P. and the executive board did just that.

After the long initial board meeting, the fire company instituted mandatory classes on sexual harassment for all members. In the past, the company had had a coed bunk room, which had never been an issue for the female members. But now a female-only bunk room was established, with locks on the inside of the door. And this bunk room was put right next to the female restroom, affording more privacy to female firefighters.

The company also spent $24,000 to have security cameras installed throughout the firehouse that alleviated blind spots and afforded better "control and accountability."

J.P. felt it necessary to do a complete and exhaustive review of the fire company's constitution, bylaws, as well as every policy and procedure, many of which dated back more than 30 years. This was to see what needed to be changed and to ensure there was an even greater system of checks and balances in place to prevent sexual misconduct from happening in the future.

Establishing transparency and communicating with the entire membership, along with the volunteer firefighting community, were two of the most important things J.P. did.

A firehouse is unlike 99.9 percent of other workplaces in the country. Across the U.S., some 69 percent of firefighters are volunteers. These volunteers work closely together in life-threatening and other high-stress emergencies, which help form a unique kind of camaraderie.

The time commitment to do the work is also enormous. Volunteer firefighters today need some 250 hours of training just to obtain certification, which can take over a year. Certifying as emergency medical technicians takes another 250 hours of training. Yet, unlike professional firefighters, volunteers don't get paid.

Since volunteer firefighters all have regular jobs, being a volunteer also takes time away from family and friends. And it's this sense of shared dedication and sacrifice, along with the ever-present danger of the job, that binds a fire company even further.

"Basically, you look at everyone here as family," J.P. Snyder said. "(Maybe) you're going to save their life, (or) they're going to save your life. You want to communicate, you want to support, you want to be there for them.

"Even the individuals we had to suspend due to the investigation, we still made sure we reached out to them on a monthly basis. We wanted to let them know we hadn't forgotten about them, that they weren't the enemy."

Nevertheless, as the weeks and months went by with still no word from the police on exactly what they were investigating, the anxiety began to take its toll on the fire company.

Membership numbers began to drop, to the point where J.P. and other officials wondered if the company would be able to provide the services it had always provided in the past.

Consideration was given to going "dual dispatch," so that the fire department down the road would be dispatched at the same time Reisterstown was, ensuring proper coverage of an emergency.

The simmering sex scandal significantly affected morale at the firehouse.

"It almost got to be like a ghost town," J.P. said. "People didn't want to be here. You always see (members) wearing their fire department T-shirts. But now there were members who didn't want to wear a Reisterstown T-shirt or sweatshirt.

"Because you didn't want to be over at Santoni's," he continued, referring to a nearby market, "getting a sub and hear 'Hey, what's going on over there?' People were embarrassed. And that's sad, when you've put all that time in this place, to be embarrassed. It was rough for a lot of people.

"There was a lot of tension. We spent countless hours in meetings. It was very stressful, because we knew we were giving a (black eye) to other volunteer fire companies. Now, people were talking about volunteer fire companies and the conduct going on, and that was embarrassing, too."

Finally, after many months, the fire company was notified by county police that the criminal probe was over, and that after consultation with the local prosecutor's office, no criminal charges would be filed.

The sense of relief among the members was palpable. But the

ripple effects of the long ordeal continued to be felt for months.

Through the fire company's Disciplinary Action Committee and administrative process, several members of the company were terminated and some severely disciplined. Leadership took a firm stance. It was time to shock the culture back into balance.

The fact that the criminal investigation was over did not automatically exonerate all of the firefighters involved. Just because they didn't do something criminally, didn't mean they upheld the standards the fire company expected. If a firefighter fails to uphold those standards, they can and should face disciplinary action, up to and including losing their membership status.

J.P. Snyder, as imperturbable as always, nevertheless shakes his head in wonder when he thinks about the turmoil that roiled the department for over seven months, all of it caused by something company officials had never foreseen: a sex scandal.

"You have to look at it as a learning experience," he said. "And the good news is, we're more prepared than ever if something like this should ever happen again."

There was no question that by taking the actions it did, the Reisterstown Volunteer Fire Company had turned short-term adversity into long-term advantage.

KEY TAKEAWAYS

1. **Gravitate to a defensible position, quickly.** What I mean by defensible is this: if anyone from the outside looking in were to critique your behavior and decision-making during a crisis—what you say, what you do, how you act—they must see that you're acting with integrity and according to policy. In other words, if anyone attempts to drag you through the court of criminal or civil law, or the court of public opinion, you need to be on the right side of an issue and in a "defensible position." Be sure you are able to articulate what you did during a crisis and why you did it,

with full justification on legal, ethical and moral grounds.

2. **Tired + wired = fired!** People under a great deal of stress stay up at night, don't get enough sleep and start to consume lots of caffeine or sugar, hoping the constant jolts will keep them going. Before they know it, their energy saps and they pull the metaphorical hand-grenade pin on themselves. Someone under crisis needs to be the same person showing-up each day—the person that is too high or too low will "slingshot" those that depend on them in ways that exacerbate the crisis and lead to unwanted attrition. J.P. did not do this. He had the perfect demeanor to weather a crisis. He was calm, level-headed and people respected him. And maybe what helped him most of all was that at the end of the day, he was able to, in his words, "leave the crisis at the firehouse" when he went home to his wife and kids.

3. **Hire a third-party expert to help you navigate crisis.** For all of the reasons mentioned previously, get some help! You wouldn't climb Mount Everest, navigate the treacherous waters of the Amazon, or fly a plane through unpredictable headwinds alone. So why would you even attempt to navigate a crisis without an experienced person who understands the nuances that will save you time, money, customers, your career, and in the worst case of scenarios, lives?

17

The Vicious Cycle of Financial Meltdown

Bert Lebhar has an opening line that just about guarantees against any yawning or checking of cell phones while he tells his story.

"Would you believe, in my career to date, I have made $69 million," he begins. "And, I don't have a pot to piss in or a window to throw it out of."

The 43-year-old president and CEO of Atlantic Remodeling, a major home improvement company based in Nottingham, Maryland, has known financial ups and downs almost from the very beginning of his existence.

As a boy, he grew up very poor. He and his mother lived in Section 8 housing in Laurel, Maryland. His mother worked three jobs to make ends meet.

"I had just an awful upbringing," he says now.

When he was 9, his house was set on fire and he was forced to jump out of the burning building from the second floor. Later, he says, the family car was blown up because his mother was a lesbian.

"I used to get the shit kicked out of me on a daily basis until I took up boxing at age 8 at the Laurel Boys and Girls Club," he says. "It saved my life."

Coming from such a hard-scrabble background, it's no surprise to hear that Lebhar did not exactly grow up financially savvy. His mother worked paycheck to paycheck, and never talked about how much money she made. No one ever explained interest rates to the boy. He never took an accounting class in high school. Make no mistake about it, his mother loves him dearly.

When he got his first credit card in college, with a $500 limit, he says he thought someone had given him $500 for free.

But by the time he reached his mid-20's, it was clear that despite all that, Lebhar had a singular gift for making money.

"People have called me *The Rainmaker*," he says, somehow managing not to sound boastful. "In fact, the only thing I'm better at than making money is spending it."

By age 26, he was a high-earning vice president of sales for a large home improvement company, making nearly $200,000 a year.

"And I was spending it all," he recalled, "because next year was always going to be better. In sales, you teach yourself if you want something and you don't have the money, you just go get more money. And I was always good at that."

But an ownership change resulted in a 30 percent pay cut for the young hotshot. Faced with another 30 percent cut shortly thereafter, he left to start his own company, Atlantic Remodeling.

Right off the bat, Lebhar says he made two strategic mistakes that would put a financial drag on his fledgling operation.

Instead of not paying himself at first or living frugally until the company was spinning off cash, he paid himself $2,000 a week to cover his monthly expenses of $7,000. And since he'd started the business with a partner, the partner was drawing the same weekly salary.

The net result was to render the company cash poor from the get-go. And as Lebhar would soon learn, asking banks for a loan was a fool's errand.

"In my business…the banks look at us like we're scum," Lebhar says. "What I've been told is that (for) banks, the bottom of the barrel would be a gentleman's club owner, a liquor store owner and a home improvement company owner. They don't want to lend money to any of those companies."

So he was forced to fund Atlantic Remodeling himself with very little access to outside cash sources, such as lines of credit, investors and Small Business Administration (SBA) loans. This would prove to be an on-going issue for 15 years.

Yet despite the long odds, Lebhar says he made money every year for 13 years—hundreds of thousands of dollars in profits.

"When that happens long enough, you develop a cowboy mentality," he says. "I remember people would tell me I should be saving for a rainy day. And my quote was: rainy days are for losers!

"I firmly believed at my ripe young age of 35, that you made your own luck. And that there was no circumstance...which I could not control. Which is unbelievably arrogant, incorrect and ignorant."

Nevertheless, Lebhar was still riding high in 2012. Atlantic Remodeling had expanded to six offices in five states across the mid-Atlantic. With 200 workers, the company was producing $12 million a year in revenue and was one of the 50 largest remodeling firms in the country.

It was winning local, regional and national awards for growth and revenue. And it's young, debonair owner was a finalist for Ernst & Young's Entrepreneur of the Year, after having won Smart CEO magazine's Circle of Excellence Award as CEO of the Year for Marketing.

Yet by the beginning of 2013, Atlantic Remodeling was edging toward a financial crisis. Lebhar says his partner began losing interest in the business. The partner had become enamored with MMA and the world of mixed martial arts. He bought a gym and training facility—his attention was passionately diverted from the business.

Because the partner's role in Atlantic Remodeling was integral (he was in charge of lead generation) business began to suffer.

Lead generation dropped to around 60 percent of where it had been. With such a dramatic drop-off, all that overhead couldn't be supported. The business almost went under, losing a half-million dollars.

The annual winter slow period that affects most home remodelers was worse than normal for Atlantic Remodeling. Spring failed to bring the usual rebound in revenue. Lebhar realized immediately how much his inattentive and unfocused partner was hurting the business—and what had to be done to fix the problem.

"But my partner was also my best friend," he says. "And that made it difficult to do what needed to be done."

By the fall of 2013, though, matters came to a head.

Lebhar realized his 50-50 partner was working half the hours he should have been working, and a third of the hours Lebhar was working. The two finally had their come-to-Jesus sit-down.

"I'm not doing this anymore," Lebhar told his partner. "Either you're leaving or I'm leaving."

But the partner didn't want the business. And Lebhar knew creditors would have stepped in and shut the company down if he himself left. So he bought the other man out.

It immediately proved to be the right move.

"Number one, I needed to show my creditors that I was taking action and I was tough enough to make the decisions that needed to be made to right the ship...," he says. "I also needed to cut costs. By cutting (his partner) and some of his friends who worked there and were collecting a paycheck, I was able to (remove) $40,000-$50,000 a month in fixed costs."

Lebhar also made changes in his own life. He and his wife were carrying a considerable amount of personal debt. And the money simply wasn't there to continue their lifestyle. Lebhar stopped paying himself a $25,000 per month salary, and focused on building his business back up.

He also made an even more dramatic decision: on the advice of bankruptcy attorneys, he stopped paying almost all his bills, except for the mortgage and utility bills for his house. Lebhar said he did this to survive.

"I stopped paying (on) my second home that my mother lived in, and my uncle," he says. "I didn't pay my credit cards, all my personal debt, unsecured debt. I haven't declared bankruptcy yet. (But) it was necessary.

". . . It ruined my credit. But I had to do it to save my business."

Now, instead of paying himself $25,000 a month, he drew a monthly salary of $7,500. And he says he was at peace with not paying his bills from a moral, ethical and legal standpoint. Lebhar believes today's onerous banking and lending laws hamstring, if not cripple, business owners like himself.

He closed two of Atlantic Remodeling branch offices but kept most of his staff, figuring staff was what he needed to produce revenue and rebuild the business. And he thought that now that a single boss was running the show, instead of two leaders with different values, beliefs and instructions, the operation would run more smoothly.

That soon proved to be the case. The very first month with Lebhar solely in charge, the company made over $50,000 in profits. And it made $50,000 in profit every month for a year.

Within a year, he says, he was current with his creditors at work. And he had $500,000 sitting in the bank.

But the rebound proved to be temporary. The executive Lebhar had hired to replace his partner brought in new managers charged with lead generation—and the results were disastrous.

In July of 2014, Atlantic Remodeling generated $850,000 in revenue. The following month, that figure cratered to $550,000, a massive 35.7 percent drop. His new right-hand man, Lebhar quickly realized, was not training the new managers properly.

In September, revenue dipped again, this time to $400,000 monthly. Lebhar fired two of the new managers. He read the riot act to his new right-hand man, eventually moving him to one of the company's remaining branches.

Meanwhile, the $500,000 that had been sitting in the bank was gone.

Again, Lebhar would blame himself for being slow to act. Perhaps his biggest mistake: he held onto unprofitable contracts for far too long out of loyalty to vendors.

"It's hard for me to separate a business relationship from a personal one," he says. "If I have a personal relationship with somebody that, let's say, I'm paying $2,500 a month to, I don't want to hurt them or their families or their income. So I'll just work harder ... and I'll keep this contract I shouldn't keep.

"I don't have the money to keep it, it's not profitable right now and my cash is dwindling and I need to sever it—but I don't *want* to. This is a weakness of mine and it's been proven for 15 years. Everyone's greatest strength is (also) everyone's greatest weakness. And I am loyal to a fault."

By the start of 2015, Lebhar says, he was back to where he'd started 15 years earlier: broke, but determined. He is a survivor.

He downsized again. March through June were good months for the business. But again, he ran into a rough patch. The business moved to a new location, but someone had failed to make sure that phone and Internet service was available.

"In the heart of my earning season, where I'm doing $500,000 a month (that's my budget), we did $248,000 in July," Lebhar said. "And I lost $100,000. Again!"

With the new location finally finished, Atlantic Remodeling rebounded yet again, doing $500,000 worth of business in both August and September. But there was another drop-off of $200,000 in October, leaving Lehbar to wonder what the future holds for the company that proudly advertises its famous "Red Cent Guarantee." ("You won't pay a red cent until the project is complete to your satisfaction.")

"There are all these outside factors that are not unique to my business," he says. "They happen to everyone's business. But it goes back to: I don't have the cash. A normal business either has a million dollars in the bank to ride these (rough periods) out, or they have access to a million dollars where they can draw on a line of credit, get through a particular crisis and move on.

"They don't have to sit down and tell their employees they can't make payroll. And, oh, by the way, work hard and do a good job these next two weeks so we can make the *next* payroll."

While Lebhar has become adept over the past 15 years at identifying what's ailing his company and fixing it, he seems weary of cycling in and out of financial difficulty.

He freely admits to spending vast sums on a lavish lifestyle that he's had to curtail to save his business, but makes no apologies for where the money went.

"I do like nice things," he says. "Growing up poor, that becomes an Achilles heel for everyone. You want to have nice things when you're young: suits, watches, cars. What I treasure more than any of that is time. And so a good majority of my money was spent on travel, leisure, food and entertainment for both myself, my friends and family."

In the meantime, as he continues shoring up his company, he's become something of an expert on ways to deal with financial stress.

His top tips? For starters: get enough sleep. At least seven hours every night.

"Sleep is something I just don't think gets talked about enough—the importance of it," he says. "You'll actually go crazy not getting enough sleep."

He also recommends spending at least a few hours a day with family.

"If you have to spend another 16 hours at work, then so be it," he says. "But if you're not spending time with your loved ones, if you're not being a husband and being a father, then what is the point of doing what you're doing? And an hour doesn't exactly get you nominated for Father of the Year."

Spend some time in solitude, too, he says, in thought and meditation and prayer. And for those new to the entrepreneurial world, he offers this: "You cannot let your business run you. You have to run your business. If it's the other way around, sirens need to go off."

His final piece of advice might also be the most basic: have a budget.

"You wouldn't believe how many people don't have a budget… or don't stick to it," he says. "If you have a budget, stick to it and put some (money) away, you'll never be in a financial crisis in the first place."

Bert Lebhar is a resilient businessman. Look for him to do great things in the future—as long as he learns from the past and follows his own advice.

KEY TAKEAWAYS

1. **Master the basics.** Family, sleep, diet, exercise, solitude and a budget…Lebhar refers to a few these pillars for success. Life balance is critical; stay on course and work your plan or you dramatically jeopardize your ability to succeed—don't waiver!

2. **Grow reserves.** The "plan for a rainy day advice" is critical for anyone. Most folks live paycheck to paycheck and their debt service far outweighs their capacity to earn. Crisis cost money and companies go out of business because they can't endure long-term legal fees, invest in sanctioned changes, pay penalties or raise capital quickly. Compounding the problems is the need to increase spending on sales and marketing to grow the top line during a critical time. Expense managing your way into profitability is a short-term proposition. Real growth is about the top line, but not all clients are good clients. Yes, cash is king and it pays to have it on hand in the event a bridge is needed.

3. **Hire the right professional service providers.** Many spend way too much money on the wrong legal team, accounting firms, insurance brokers, IT professionals, managerial

consultants and other outside service providers. The aggrieved are often upset and contemplate lawsuits. Remember, terminate relationships with care as lawsuits are long-term and expensive. And each lawsuit can have an equal and opposite reaction. Always protect your reputation—it has value!

4. **No one truly thinks like the owner, except the owner!** No matter how much you incent financially or motivate emotionally, no one you ever hire will truly be invested in your business like you, the owner. Know it, accept it and make decisions accordingly.

5. **Decide objectively, not emotionally.** Many in business tolerate mediocrity and fail to make hard decisions because they (1) hope negative behavior will change with a sound pep talk or incentives and (2) fear having the tough conversations which create transition. Lebhar talks about not wanting to negatively impact someone else at his own peril—all of his cash reserves were nearly drained before firing anyone. Make the tough decisions, quickly, for the sake of the business and those who are motivated to succeed. Find the competent, motivated people who don't mind change and adversity—they will be at your side during the toughest days. Reward their loyalty and performance.

6. **Mission work is important.** Throughout Lebhar's career, he has made time to give to charitable causes, particularly in support of homelessness. There are many ways to give—time, money, in-kind services, etc. Figure-out what is important to you and become an even stronger presence in the social fabric of your community.

Final Thoughts...

- There are two kinds of people in this world...those who give you energy and those who take it away. Which one are you and with whom do you surround yourself?

- When someone comes to you with a problem, you have one of two buckets to pour—one full of gasoline and one full of water. Do you ignite issues and make matters worse or resolve conflict and create optimal outcomes?

- When faced with an urgent situation, slow the process down and act non-emotionally. People often want to react with the same velocity with which crisis hits—do not. Slow the process down and make sound decisions that will benefit for many years to come.

- "It takes 20 years to build a reputation and five minutes to ruin it. If you think about that, you'll do things differently" What crisis leadership contribution would be worth its salt without quoting Warren Buffett?

- When running-up against difficult people, take the high road! Remember, when you roll around with the pigs in the mud, the pigs like it and you get dirty (my favorite iteration of a George

Bernard Shaw quotation).

- When faced with intense professional scrutiny, there is one piece of advice that generally cures a lot of ills—just win! Over-deliver on your goals, whatever they may be: sales, profitability, growth, promotion, etc. People want to be around winners.

- Accelerate your mistakes. When you've made a bad decision, cycle through it as quickly as possible—right the ship.

- Hire and lead motivated people. There is no time to try and motivate a person who doesn't want to succeed more than you want them to. Hire slow, fire fast!

- Every time you advantage one person, you disadvantage another. Treat people fairly and equitably. By the way, fairly doesn't necessarily mean the same.

- Great mentors are able to teach, communicate, motivate, empower and instill a sense of accountability among the people they lead. It's all about personal and professional trust.

- It's not what you take on, it's what you accomplish!

- Give to others—you're never standing taller than when you're bending over helping someone else.

- Never lose your insatiable thirst for knowledge and always be curious—you're never too old to learn or reinvent yourself.

- "I've learned that people will forget what you said, people will forget what you did, but people will never forget how you made them feel."—Maya Angelou.

- When all is said and done, what do you want to have said and done? When you figure that out, do it!

About the Authors

Robert W. Weinhold, Jr., Chief Executive | Fallston Group, LLC

After decades of private and public sector leadership service, Rob Weinhold continued his career mission of helping organizations during life's most critical times by launching Fallston Group (www.fallstongroup.com) in 2009. Fallston Group is a Baltimore-based crisis management and strategic communications firm designed to help organizations and individuals build, strengthen and defend their reputations. Throughout his distinguished career, Rob has worked on the core executive leadership team at all three levels of government and privately on Major League Baseball Hall of Famer Cal Ripken Jr.'s core executive team in Baltimore, Maryland. During his time at Ripken Baseball, Rob oversaw all aspects of Cal's core amateur sports business, including sales, marketing, business development, sponsorships, brand experience, operations and design/build efforts. He led the vision to develop the organization's first out-of-state amateur sports presence in Myrtle Beach, South Carolina.

During his public service career, Rob most notably served in a sworn capacity for the Baltimore Police Department and was ultimately promoted to Public Affairs Director. He also served as Chief of Staff for the United States Department of Justice and senior executive within Maryland's Governor's Office. While in these roles, Rob also served as chief spokesperson for the entities he represented; he has conducted thousands of media interviews and is thought of as an expert communications strategist. Rob has been an on-air contributor for CNN, FOX, MSNBC and many other national and locally affiliated media outlets. He is referred to as a crisis leadership expert.

Rob maintains extensive experience in the areas of executive leadership, organizational strategy, crisis management and communications, reputation management, media relations, marketing communications, public affairs, business management and operations. His clients often refer to Rob as their CRO—Chief Reputation Officer—as he operates at the critical intersection of leadership, strategy and communications.

Rob earned his graduate degree (MSM) from The Johns Hopkins University and undergraduate degree from the University of Baltimore. Rob is nationally published and has trained and lectured in a variety of professional and academic settings. His new book, *The Art of Crisis Leadership*, is scheduled for publication in April 2016. Rob travels from the United States of America.

Kevin Cowherd

Kevin Cowherd is the author, along with Hall of Famer Cal Ripken Jr., of the New York Times best-seller "Hothead" and five other baseball novels for young readers. Their sixth book, "The Closer," was published by Disney-Hyperion in March. Cowherd's last two non-fiction books for Apprentice House Press were "The Opening Act: Comedy, Life and the Desperate Pursuit of Happiness," a look at the career of Baltimore comic Larry Noto, and "Hale Storm: The Incredible Saga of Baltimore's Ed Hale, Including a Secret Life with the CIA."

Cowherd was an award-winning sports and features columnist for *The Baltimore Sun* for 32 years and has also written for *Men's Health*, *Parenting* and *Baseball Digest* magazines. A collection of his newspaper columns, "Last Call at the 7-Eleven" can still be found in fine remainder bins everywhere.

He lives in northern Baltimore County with his wife, Nancy.

Apprentice House is the country's only campus-based, student-staffed book publishing company. Directed by professors and industry professionals, it is a nonprofit activity of the Communication Department at Loyola University Maryland.

Using state-of-the-art technology and an experiential learning model of education, Apprentice House publishes books in untraditional ways. This dual responsibility as publishers and educators creates an unprecedented collaborative environment among faculty and students, while teaching tomorrow's editors, designers, and marketers.

Outside of class, progress on book projects is carried forth by the AH Book Publishing Club, a co-curricular campus organization supported by Loyola University Maryland's Office of Student Activities.

Eclectic and provocative, Apprentice House titles intend to entertain as well as spark dialogue on a variety of topics. Financial contributions to sustain the press's work are welcomed. Contributions are tax deductible to the fullest extent allowed by the IRS.

To learn more about Apprentice House books or to obtain submission guidelines, please visit www.apprenticehouse.com.

Apprentice House
Communication Department
Loyola University Maryland
4501 N. Charles Street
Baltimore, MD 21210
Ph: 410-617-5265 • Fax: 410-617-2198
info@apprenticehouse.com • www.apprenticehouse.com

CPSIA information can be obtained
at www.ICGtesting.com
Printed in the USA
BVHW031455310321
603814BV00005B/524/J